Conten·

Marie's Story

Helping people achieve their dreams is one way to describe Marie Griffiths' vocation in life. When she opened her first Slimtone class in 1982, she never imagined how big an impact this would have on so many people. Now running 20 classes in South Wales, Marie's approach to losing weight and getting fit has always been one of friendly encouragement, supported by diet plans based on 'real' food and up to the minute nutritional information. As Marie says "my intention has always been to help people help themselves. Our classes are attended by people of all shapes and sizes who are all looking for the same thing – lasting weight loss and improved health. Together we create an atmosphere which is fun but informative – no faddy foods, no expensive supplements, just sensible eating plans and each others' support." The success stories on the Slimtone website speak for themselves – hundreds of men and women who by losing weight (and keeping it off) have given themselves the key to unlocking their potential.

Hello, I'm Marie Griffiths

Welcome to Slimtone!

If you are looking for friendly advice, support and a Healthy Lifestyle, you have just taken a step in the right direction.

The Lifestyle Plan is designed for people with busy lives who love good food. My experience with hundreds of men and women has proven that a simple, easy to follow plan that fits into everyone's lifestyle is the key to Slimtone's success.

You won't be hungry, you won't be bored but you will lose weight. Together with an enjoyable exercise programme as recommended in the plan, you will soon be enjoying the healthy lifestyle that you have always dreamed of.

Best wishes

Marie

P.S. If you are looking for a quicker weight loss, choose the low G.I. recommendations ☺ to Jumpstart your healthier lifestyle.

Slimtone's Lifestyle Plan

Losing weight couldn't be easier with your Lifestyle Plan. It's been designed to provide balanced healthy eating without leaving you feeling deprived.

Simply follow the guidelines, recipes and suggestions and you will soon be enjoying a steady, healthy and permanent weight loss. You can mix 'n' match the six week menu plans to suit your lifestyle. You will soon discover it takes all the effort out of dieting. When your weight loss needs a "JUMPSTART" follow the low G.I. meals and ideas suggested in the plan. ☺

Guidelines to your plan

The Lifestyle Plan has been designed to change the way we think about food. It offers a healthy option for all situations – including snacks, packed lunches, and even eating out and takeaways. These can all now be enjoyed following our guidelines. It takes the guesswork out of counting calories. The low fat recipes and meal suggestions follow the current nutritional guidelines for a balanced healthy eating diet.

1. Be organised

Design your own personal Lifestyle Plan. Read through the meals and recipes highlighting your favourites. This will enable you to plan your meals at a glance. Being organised is the key to success and the Slimtone motto is FAILING TO PLAN IS PLANNING TO FAIL…

2. Check portions

Weigh and measure the suggested portions to get your daily nutritional requirement. The amount of food stated has been precisely calculated for maximum weight loss. It also helps prevent those hunger pangs so often experienced on a diet.

3. Take a 'before' photograph

Have a photograph taken at the start of your Lifestyle Plan. This is a great way to see what you've achieved. So many of our members have regretted not having this priceless possession when they reach their ideal weight.

4. Inch loss chart

After your weekly weigh in, complete your weight and inch loss on the record sheet provided. You will find that watching the inches as well as the pounds disappear will provide you with the necessary motivation on those inevitable 'down' days.

5. Daily food planner

Get into the habit of planning and organising your meals from your Lifestyle Plan on your daily food diary. This way you are in control of food – not your food in control of you. Diet at a standstill? List all the foods you 'pick' daily in your diary in red (yes, even cold chips and broken biscuits have calories) you will soon discover the plan works when you do.

6. Weekly shopping list

The shopping list provides a comprehensive guide to all the Slimtone recommended products. Also ideas to include variety in your diet and prevent the inevitable boredom that can sometimes ruin the best of intentions.

How it works

LADIES:

Less than two stone to lose   1250 calories daily

Select your meals from the suggestions in your Lifestyle Plan or the "Six Week Programme". (You will notice these have been colour coded for your convenience) If you need a Jumpstart look for the low G.I. ☺ ideas.

Breakfast
Lunch
Main Meal
Snack Meal or Treat (as suggested in plan or up to 250 cals per day)

Over two stone to lose   1500 calories daily

As above but include a snack meal and treat each day.

MEN AND TEENAGERS:

Less than two stone to lose   1500 calories daily

Make your personal choice as above.

For men and teenagers with more than two stone to lose make your choice as above and include a further snack meal.

Lifestyle Plan Daily Allowances (approx 200 cals)

The following are an important part of your plan. They provide calcium, vitamins and minerals essential for a healthy diet.

- ½ pint skimmed/semi-skimmed/soya/rice milk
- Two portions of fruit and unlimited vegetables from Take '5' Selection.

Drinks:

Tea and decaffeinated coffee can be used freely with milk from your allowance. You can also use low calorie drinks, fruit or herbal teas and non-carbonated mineral water.

Water is an essential part of your Lifestyle Plan.

IT IS IMPORTANT YOU DRINK 6–8 GLASSES OF WATER DAILY (approximately 2 litres) A slice of lemon, lime, fresh orange or a splash of lemon juice can be added to enhance the flavour.

(Find out why it is so important to include water on page 66 of your plan)

Lifestyle Plan

Your Lifestyle Plan has been designed following the guidelines for a balanced healthy eating diet. Follow the guidelines below for maximum nutrition.

Take '5' selection.

Always eat a minimum of five portions of FRUIT AND VEGETABLES a day from your Take '5' Selection. They provide fibre, water, vitamins and minerals all of which are vital for good health.

Get hooked on fish.

Eat at least three servings a week of the following oily fish – salmon, mackerel, herrings, sardines, fresh tuna, and trout. These are the richest sources of the 'healthy fat' omega 3. This essential fat is needed to support mood, memory and concentration, a healthy heart, hormonal balance, healthy skin and joints and weight management.

☺ Jumpstart Your Lifestyle Plan.

The following options will provide you with low G.I. foods. Together with the ideas in your plan you will have the perfect recipe for success. They provide slow release energy and satisfy your appetite for a longer period of time, preventing those dreaded hunger pangs and making you less inclined to look for quick fix snacks.

- BREAD: Multigrain, seeded, granary or wholemeal is recommended, also wholemeal pitta bread and tortilla wraps.
- CEREALS: Wholegrain breakfast cereals, bran-based cereals, porridge and no added sugar muesli.
- POTATOES: Sweet potatoes and boiled new potatoes in skins.
- PASTA: Preferably wholemeal. Pasta has a lower G.I. than potatoes and rice.
- RICE: Brown rice and basmati rice has a lower G.I. than other rice.
- FRUITS: Grapes and watermelon are high G.I fruits so limit these and avoid over ripe bananas, which have a higher G.I. rating. Apples and pears with the skin, peaches, plums, mango and cherries are good choices for lower G.I fruits.
- VEGETABLES: Most vegetables are Low G.I, with the exception of peas, sweetcorn and pumpkin so limit these. Beansprouts, tomatoes, courgettes and celery are all very low G.I. and great for "bulking out" your Lifestyle Plan recipes.

Take '5' Selection

Aim to eat at least five portions of fruit and vegetables a day as recommended by the Department of Health. A portion is approximately 80g (2¾oz).

Lifestyle Plan Fruit Basket

Make your selection from the following. Use fresh, frozen, dried or canned fruit in natural juice NOT syrup and 100% pure unsweetened juice.
One Portion = One large slice melon or fresh pineapple – ½ grapefruit – 1 medium apple – orange – pear – peach – nectarine – 2 satsumas – 2 kiwis – a handful of grapes 84g (3oz) – 4 plums – 168g (6oz) soft fruit (e.g. blueberries, blackberries, raspberries, strawberries etc.) – 1small banana – 150ml (4 fl oz) **unsweetened** fruit juice (e.g. orange, grapefruit, cranberry etc.) – 3 ready dried apricots or prunes – 1 level tablespoon of sultanas, raisins or currants – rhubarb is so low in calories it can be eaten in unlimited quantities.

Lifestyle Plan Vegetable Basket

It is essential that you include a selection of vegetables from the 'Vegetable Basket' in your daily plan. They are low in fat, high in fibre and rich in many other valuable nutrients. They also have a high water content, which satisfies the appetite with a minimum of calories. The following can be eaten in unlimited quantities, enjoy lightly boiled, steamed, stir-fried, roasted or as a side salad. These can be fresh, canned or frozen.

Artichokes – asparagus – aubergines – beansprouts – beetroot – broccoli – brussel sprouts – butternut squash - cabbage – carrots – cauliflower – celery – chicory – chives – courgettes – cucumber – endives – runner/green beans – kale - leeks – lettuce – marrow – mushrooms – mustard and cress – mange-tout – onions – parsley – peppers – pumpkin – radish – rocket - spinach – spring greens – spring onions – sugar snap peas - swede – Swiss chard - tomatoes – turnips – watercress.

The following vegetables can be included in your menus, and the calories deducted from your daily 'treat' allowance.

Per 15 ml/tblspn approx. 28g (1oz)
Broad beans, parsnips and peas 15 cals
Sweetcorn 30 cals
Potatoes 28g (1oz) approx. 20 cals
Sweet Potatoes 28g (1oz) approx. 24 cals

See our vegetable recipes and ideas on page 48.

Breakfast or Snack Meal (approx. 200 cals)

It is essential that you <u>do not skip breakfast</u>, as it is the most important meal of the day! It has been show n that people who skip breakfast are actually likely to have an overall higher calorie intake throughout the day. A selection from your plan provides you with the slow release energy required to prevent those mid-morning hunger pangs.

Select any one of the following:

Quick and Easy Breakfasts

(Any of the fruit stated in the suggestions below are in addition to your daily allowance)

1. 28g (1oz) of wholegrain cereal / porridge topped with a small sliced banana or 28g (1oz) raisins with milk from allowance.

2. 42g (1½oz) (dry weight) porridge oats cooked in water, served with milk from allowance, topped with sliced strawberries / blueberries and 1 pot low fat yoghurt.

3. 2 Weetabix/Shredded Wheat topped with small sliced banana and served with milk from allowance.

4. Small tin of grapefruit segments in own juice followed by 28g (1oz) of your favourite breakfast cereal served with milk from your allowance.

5. 28g (1oz) wholegrain breakfast cereal/porridge oats mixed with 28g (1oz) muesli and served with milk from allowance.

6. 112g (4oz) strawberries and 112g (4oz) chopped melon topped with 28g (1oz) no added sugar muesli and 1 pot low fat yoghurt 140g (5oz) or fromage frais.
☺ any type except watermelon

7. 1 small can of fruit salad in natural juice (or three portions of fruit from Fruit Basket) served with low fat yoghurt or fromage frais.

8. Toast 2 crumpets and serve with 2 low fat cheese triangles and thin spread of Marmite or 2 tspns low fat spread and 2 tspns reduced sugar jam.

9. Toast 1 muffin or small teacake and serve with 2 tspns reduced sugar jam or marmalade.

10. 1 small wholemeal bagel served with 2 tspns reduced sugar jam.

11. 1 crusty wholemeal or granary roll or small wedge of French loaf served with 1 individual Pick 'n' Mix cheese or low fat cheese slice.

12. Toast one side only of a thin slice of wholemeal bread. Heat 140g (5oz) baked beans and spoon onto un-toasted side of bread. Grate or thinly slice 28g (1oz) low fat cheddar-type cheese and place on top of beans. Place under pre-heated grill until cheese has melted. Serve with sliced tomato.

13. Strawberry Smoothie – Blend approx. 6 large strawberries, 1/3 pint (300 mls) of cold milk and a small pot of low fat strawberry yoghurt. Serve chilled.

MARIE'S TOP TIP :

√ Smoothies make an ideal breakfast in a hurry. Any of the fruit in the plan are ideal.

Tasty Toast Topper Selection

Toast 1 slice of wholemeal bread from a large thick-sliced loaf and serve with any of the following:

1. Spread toast with fruit sauce and top with a rasher grilled lean bacon and poached egg.

2. 1 medium-sized egg poached, boiled or scrambled. Serve with grilled tomatoes and mushrooms.

3. Small can of baked beans with poached mushrooms and grilled tomatoes.

4. Top toast with small carton of low fat cottage cheese and sliced tomato, pop under hot grill and serve.

5. One medium banana mashed with 1 tspn of honey (optional).

6. Toast bread on one side only. Top with two mashed sardines (canned in tomato sauce or brine) and season with balsamic vinegar. Pop under hot grill.

Toast 2 slices wholemeal bread from a large medium-sliced loaf and serve with any of the following:

1. 28g (1oz) low fat paté, grilled tomato and mushrooms

2. 2 low fat cheese triangles / Marmite.

3. 2 tspns reduced sugar jam or marmalade.

4. 56g (2oz) Extra Light Cream cheese.

5. Simmer a can of chopped tomatoes, season with herbs and serve with Slimtone garlic mushrooms.

MARIE'S TOP TIP

√ Remove leftovers from plates immediately to avoid any temptation to pick.

REMEMBER LITTLE PICKERS WEAR BIG KNICKERS...

All-Day Cooked Breakfasts

1. Grill 3 turkey rashers as directed. Serve with 1 poached egg, grilled tomatoes, Slimtone garlic mushrooms and 1 thin slice of bread toasted.

2. 2 small well-grilled low fat sausages, 1 well-grilled back rasher bacon, served with tomatoes and mushrooms.

3. Halve 1 wholemeal muffin. Toast and sandwich together with 1 small poached egg and 28g (1oz) wafer-thin ham.

4. Grill 1 Potato Waffle and top with poached or scrambled egg. Serve with grilled tomatoes and mushrooms.

MARIE'S TOP TIP

√ Simply add 140g (5 oz) of Slimtone 'fried potatoes' for a tasty and filling lunch.

'Two For The Price Of One' Breakfast

I have included the following suggestions enabling you to 'split' your breakfast/snack into two meals. This is a really convenient breakfast for early risers and will also provide a mid morning snack.

Select two from the list below....

1. 28g (1oz) porridge oats made up with water and served with milk from allowance.

2. 1 Weetabix with ½ medium banana and milk from allowance.

3. 1 medium slice wholemeal toast spread with remainder of banana.

4. 28g (1oz) favourite breakfast cereal served with milk from allowance

5. 1 large banana or 2 pieces of fruit from the fruit bowl.

6. 1 small can grapefruit segments/ fruit salad in natural juice.

7. 1 200g pot low fat yoghurt or cereal bar up to 100 cals.

8. 1 thick slice wholemeal toast topped with:
   a. Low fat cheese triangle and Marmite.
   b. Grilled or canned tomatoes served with poached mushrooms.
   c. Two tspns reduced sugar jam/marmalade.

Easy Meals for Busy Days (approx. 300 cals)

The following low fat options are ideal for a quick snack, light lunch or evening meal and are both tasty and easy to prepare. Select one from the following suggestions and serve with unlimited cooked or stir-fried vegetables, side salad or large portion of Slimtone coleslaw. When selecting meals from the plan, the fat and calorie content have been calculated for you.

Tasty Jacket Potato

Cook one medium sized jacket potato (approx. 224g (8oz) uncooked weight) - Serve with unlimited salad or stir-fry vegetables and filled with any of the following.

☺ Try substituting the jacket potato for a baked, medium sized sweet potato. They're higher in fibre, vitamins and minerals and lower G.I

1. 28g (1oz) grated medium fat cheddar cheese and 1 tblspn sweet pickle.

2. 112g (4oz) low fat cottage cheese (any flavour).

3. 56g (2oz) prawns or 2 crab sticks mixed with 1 tblspn low fat mayonnaise or reduced calorie thousand island dressing.

4. Dice 56g (2oz) lean cooked chicken into bite-sized pieces. Mix 2 level tspns mild curry paste with Slimtone coleslaw. Stir in chicken together with diced cucumber, red or yellow pepper, and season with freshly ground black pepper.

5. Small can of tuna in brine or spring water (drained) mixed with 1 tblspn low fat mayonnaise and diced cucumber.

6. 1 small can of baked beans For extra flavour add curry or chilli powder.
☺ Reduced sugar and salt when possible.

7. 1 hardboiled egg chopped, mixed with diced cucumber and 1 tblspn low fat mayonnaise.

8. Large portion Slimtone coleslaw mixed with 28g (1oz) grated medium fat cheddar cheese or prawns.

9. Large portion of Slimtone soup with 56g (2oz) cubed corned beef.

10. Grill 1 slice of lean back bacon and snip into bite-sized pieces. Remove filling from potato, mix with bacon, chopped cherry tomatoes and chives. Pop back into potato and top with a poached egg.

Slimtone Potato Wedges

Alternatively, a nutritious and tasty snack meal can be made in just a few minutes by cooking potato wedges and topping with any of the suggested fillings for jacket potatoes.

Slice potato into 8 wedges. Place in a microwave dish with tblspn water and cover. Cook on full power for 8 mins. Spray wedges with low fat cooking spray and place under pre heated grill until crisp. Flavour with garlic, paprika, dry chilli flakes or 'all purpose' seasoning before grilling.

MARIE'S TOP TIP

☺ Sweet potatoes make delicious wedges, they are also low G.I., tasty when boiled or roasted.
√ Great with a dip of extra light mayo.

Sandwiches, Wraps and Baps

For a tasty snack or packed lunch select one of the following Slimtone ideas for sandwich fillings. They make a nutritious and delicious meal; enjoy them with a large salad, Slimtone coleslaw or a satisfying portion of Slimtone soup

Use any ONE of the following:

- 2 slices wholemeal/granary bread from medium sliced loaf.
- 1 medium size wholemeal/granary bap
- 1 panini/bread wrap/wholemeal pitta bread.

1. Spread bread with one low fat cheese triangle, low fat salad cream or extra light mayonnaise. Fill with 56g (2oz) wafer thin cooked ham, chicken or turkey etc., followed by one selection from the 'Fruit Basket' or low fat yoghurt.

2. Spread bread with brown sauce and fill with 28g (1oz) grated medium fat cheddar cheese mixed with grated carrot and shredded lettuce. Serve with 1 packet low fat crisps.

3. Spread bread with low fat mayonnaise. Fill with small can of tuna in brine or 56g (2oz) canned salmon, top with sliced beefsteak tomato, rocket and spring onions.

4. Mix together 56g (2oz) prawns or crab sticks, coriander, black pepper and lime juice. Spread bread with extra light mayonnaise, top with shredded lettuce, and fill with prawn mix.

5. Spread bread with brown sauce/ tomato ketchup, fill with two cooked turkey rashers and one medium-sized, chopped, hard boiled egg.

6. Spread bread with extra light mayonnaise or salad dressing. Fill with 28g (1oz) grated cheese, wafer thin ham and canned pineapple. (Delicious toasted in health grill)

7. 1 small pot of paste or 56g (2oz) low fat paté, 1 low fat yoghurt.

8. Mix 1 tblspn extra light mayo with a little mango chutney and spread over bread. Fill with 56g (2oz) ready-cooked chicken Tikka mini fillets and lots of crunchy salad.

9. Mix together 56g (2oz) low fat cottage cheese, 28g (1oz) grated medium fat cheddar cheese. Add finely chopped celery, grated carrot and beansprouts.

10. Make up raita by mixing extra light mayonnaise, mint sauce, coriander, cucumber, spring onion and natural yoghurt. Spread over bread and fill with 56g (2oz) Tandoori chicken pieces.

11. Mix together 1 tblspn Mexican hot salsa sauce with 1 tblspn extra light mayonnaise, stir in 56g (2oz) chopped chicken, spread mixture on bread with rocket or baby spinach leaves and sandwich together.

12. Spread bread with low fat cheese triangle, fill with 56g (2oz) beetroot and lots of salad, serve with 1 packet low fat crisps.

13. 1 hard boiled, medium-sized egg, mashed with 1 tblspn of low fat mayonnaise (optional), cress, sliced tomato and shredded iceberg lettuce.

14. Spread bread with low fat cream cheese. Fill with rocket, chopped cherry tomatoes and two grilled turkey rashers. Season with black pepper.

15. Spread wrap with pesto sauce. Fill with 84g (3oz) chicken tikka fillets, cherry tomatoes and rocket leaves .

16. Spread bread with 2 tblspn of reduced fat houmous, add baby spinach or rocket leaves and sliced mixed peppers.

17. Pre-packed sandwich up to 300 calories and 12g fat.

MARIE'S TOP TIP

√ A toastie always makes a satisfying snack. Pop any of the above into your health grill and enjoy.

√ Keep wraps and pitta bread fresh for lunch by wrapping in foil.

Corned Beef Recipes

The following are a selection of Slimtone's favourite corned beef recipes; they can be prepared quickly and enjoyed by all the family. Always use low fat, premium corned beef. Also, frozen sliced onions are ideal for convenience in these recipes.

Corned Beef Rissoles

Mix 56g (2oz) corned beef with 112g (4oz) mashed potato and cooked onion and carrot. Make into 2 rissoles and 'fry' in non-stick pan. Serve with 112g (4oz) fresh or frozen peas, lots of free vegetables and Slimtone gravy.

MARIE'S TOP TIP

√ Always add corned beef to cold potato mixture as this prevents rissoles from breaking when cooking.

Corned Beef Gravy

Simmer 1 small chopped onion until soft, add 2 heaped tspns of gravy granules and 84g (3oz) corned beef. Simmer gently for 10 mins. Serve with 140g (5oz) boiled potatoes and free vegetables from 'Vegetable Basket'.

Corned Beef Casserole

Cook 1 small chopped onion, add 56g (2oz) cubed corned beef and 112g (4oz) boiled potato. Transfer to shallow dish and cover with 28g (1oz) medium fat grated cheese and 1 sliced tomato. Grill until cheese is melted. Serve with unlimited selection from 'Vegetable Basket'.

Corned Beef Savoury Slice

Mash 1 large can corned beef with 1 small grated onion and press mixture into base of an ovenproof dish. Beat two large eggs, with 1 cup semi skimmed milk and season. Pour over the corned beef mixture. Top with green and red peppers and sliced mushrooms. Place in a moderate oven for approx. 25 mins or until set. Serve hot or cold with a large salad.

Corned Beef Hash

Boil 140g (5oz) potatoes, 1 chopped onion and 2 diced carrots until cooked. Mash together with 84g (3oz) corned beef. Serve with Slimtone gravy and 'free veg'.

Baked Bean Hotpot

Chop small onion and simmer in salted water with 112g (4oz) mixed peas and carrots for 5 mins. Drain, cut 56g (2oz) corned beef into cubes and place in the pan with vegetables, 1 small can of baked beans and 2 tblspns brown sauce. Heat through and serve with unlimited vegetables from 'Vegetable Basket'.

Corned Beef Quiche

Serves 4 – approx. 250 cals- 12g fat per portion
Beat 4 eggs and 224g (8oz) carton of cottage cheese in basin with seasoning. Slice large can of corned beef and layer in 2" deep x approx 10" wide dish and alternate with chopped onion, mushrooms, cooked mixed vegetables and cottage cheese/eggs mixture as if making lasagne. Place final layer of cheese mix on top and cover with sliced tomato. Cook in moderate oven for approx 30 minutes.

MARIE'S TOP TIP
√ For convenience use 113g (4oz) frozen mixed vegetables.

Corned Beef Toastie

Mash 56g (2oz) corned beef with finely shredded onion, fill two medium slices granary bread, pop into health grill and garnish with sliced tomatoes.

Corned Beef & Onion Jacket

Cook a 224g (8oz) potato. Scoop out potato and mash with 56g (2oz) corned beef finely diced onion and cherry tomatoes. Return filling to jacket and bake in the oven for 10 minutes.

Corned Beef Savoury Baskets

Makes 40 – approx 79 cals each - 3.1g fat

Pastry:

450g (1 lb) self raising flour	pinch of salt
196g (7oz) half fat butter	½ of cup of water

Filling:

1 large onion	224g (8oz) potatoes
2 tspns Worcester sauce	224g (8oz) swede
1 x 340g (12oz) can of corned beef	

Sieve flour and salt into mixing bowl and rub in butter until resembling fine breadcrumbs. Add water as necessary to bind together. Roll out thinly on a lightly floured surface. Using a 3" cutter make into 40 baskets, place onto patty tin, which has been lightly misted with low fat cooking spray.

FILLING: Boil onion, potatoes and swede in lightly salted water until cooked. Mash together with corned beef. Add Worcester sauce and season to taste. Place one heaped tblspn of mixture into each individual pastry basket. Cut remaining pastry with a different shaped cutter (e.g. star) and place on top of filling. Cook for 12–15 minutes at 180°C/375°F/Gas Mark 6.

MARIE'S TOP TIP

√ This is an ideal recipe for buffets.

MARIE'S TOP TIP

√ For convenience divide a can of corned beef into four portions and freeze. You will find this really useful for making up your easy meals for busy days.

Soup

Soup is one of those foods that make us satisfied without lots of 'empty calories'. The following recipes are a selection of Slimtone favourites, which all make a tasty starter to a meal. Also, they are the perfect healthy option for a snack or packed meal.

Cream of Broccoli Soup

Serves 4 - 65 cals – neg fat per serving
Stir fry 1 small diced potato, 2 heads of broccoli, and 1 small chopped onion for 1-2 mins. Add 1½ pints of chicken stock (made with two stock cubes) and 1 tspn dried basil. Bring to the boil and then simmer for 20-30 mins. Allow to cool. Liquidise and stir in 1 small can evaporated low fat milk. This recipe also makes a delicious sauce for poultry or fish.

MARIE'S TOP TIP

√ Mushrooms, carrots or courgettes make a tasty alternative to broccoli.

Leek & Potato Soup

Serves 4 - 80 cals – 1.3g fat per serving
Stir-fry 2 large leeks, 2 medium diced potatoes, and 1 chopped onion for 1-2 mins. Add 1 ½ pints of chicken stock (made with 2 stock cubes). Bring to the boil and simmer gently for 20-30 mins. Add fresh parsley halfway through. Allow to cool and liquidise. Stir in a small can of evaporated low fat milk or low fat fromage frais.

MARIE'S TOP TIP

√ Sweet potatoes can also be used in this recipe ☺.

Ham & Pea Soup

Serves 1 - 300 cals – 1.3g fat per serving
Make up stock with one ham flavoured stock cube and 1 pint of water. Simmer 56g (2oz) dried marrowfat peas, with a selection of free vegetables and 2 smoked lean and low bacon rashers cooked and finely sliced. Serve with slice of bread or 140g (5oz) potatoes.

Cream of Vegetable Soup

Serves 4 – approx.40 cals – neg. fat per serving
Make a large quantity of Slimtone Super Soup. Liquidise half of the soup and return to the pan. Add a small can of low fat evaporated milk and garnish with parsley before serving.

Sweet Potato Soup

Serves 4 – approx 175 cals - 1.2g fat per serving.

1 onion, chopped
2 cloves garlic, crushed
650g (1½lb) sweet potato, peeled and chopped
1 large red pepper, deseeded and chopped
1.2 litres of vegetable stock (2 stock cubes)
1 small can of low fat evaporated milk

Mist large saucepan with cooking spray and cook onion for 2 minutes. Add garlic and cook for a further minute, then stir in potato, pepper and stock. Bring to the boil, simmer for approx. 15 mins. Blitz with hand held blender, add milk, season with salt and freshly ground black pepper.

Butternut Squash Soup

Serves 2 – approx 75 cals – Neg fat per serving

1 butternut squash
1 clove garlic, chopped
600ml water
2 vegetable stock cubes
pinch of nutmeg
pinch of black pepper

Peel the butternut squash and remove the seeds. Dice the squash. Mist non stick pan with low fat cooking spray and sauté squash with the garlic for 3-4 minutes. Add the water, stock cubes, nutmeg, black pepper and simmer for 15 minutes (until the squash is tender). Blend the soup. Serve (use a swirl of yoghurt and a pinch of nutmeg for optional decoration)

MARIE'S TOP TIP

√ Avoid buying ready prepared croutons as they can be high in fat content.

√ Try our tasty recipe. Cut bread into cubes and place on a baking tray. Spray with low cal cooking spray, season with garlic, paprika etc, and oven bake until crisp. These are ideal with soups or salad.

Beetroot Soup

Serves 2 – approx 50 cals – 2g fat per serving

4 beetroots, uncooked, peeled and sliced
1 tspn olive oil
1 red onion
2 cloves garlic
2 vegetable stock cubes
400ml (11 fl oz) water
1 tspn dried thyme
100ml (3 fl oz) semi-skimmed milk
Black pepper and a pinch of salt

Fry the onions and garlic until brown. Add the stock and the sliced beetroot, thyme and pepper. Simmer until beetroot is soft (around 20 mins). Either liquidize or use a potato masher to make a chunky and filling soup. Add the milk. Serve with a swirl of yoghurt and thyme to garnish.

Easy Lentil Soup

Serves 4 – approx 220 cals – neg fat per serving

Medium sized bag of red lentils, approx 10 oz (280 g)
2 leeks
1 onion
2 vegetable stock cubes
Black pepper
Herbs of choice to taste

Rinse the lentils in cold water and drain. Place in large saucepan and top with boiled water (about 3/4 full) and boil for 10 minutes. Meanwhile thickly chop the onion and leeks and add to the lentils. Mix the stock cubes with boiling water in a jug until dissolved and add this along with black pepper and herbs. Simmer on a medium heat for 45 mins or until the lentils are soft. Liquidise and serve.

MARIE'S TOP TIP
√ Add any of your free vegetables from your Take '5' Selection to make a tasty and satisfying soup i.e. carrots, swede, etc.

MARIE'S TOP TIP
√ Make your own garlic bread by topping one small crusty roll with two tspns of low fat spread. Sprinkle with garlic, cover with foil and place in a hot oven for 5 minutes.

Slimtone Super Soup

The following recipe is one of the most popular with Slimtone members. It's a tasty starter and a nourishing snack or packed meal.

Simmer in stock cube a selection of free vegetables e.g. carrots, swedes, leeks, onions, parsley, celery, beansprouts etc. When cooked liquidise half of the soup and return to the remaining vegetables making it thicker and more satisfying.

Make a tasty calorie free vegetable curry sauce by liquidising the soup and adding curry powder to taste. Or alternatively add gravy granules and use as 'free' gravy.

Variations can be made quite easily with the following:

84g (3oz) corned beef 183 cals
112g (4oz) parsnips 64 cals
Lentils, split peas 81 cals per 28g (1oz) dry weight
Potatoes 20 cals per 28g (1oz)
Gravy granules 19 cals per 100 ml serving

Cauliflower and Stilton Soup

Serves 4 – approx 216 cals - 12g fat per serving

1 large cauliflower
2 medium onions, chopped
1 garlic clove, crushed
1 vegetable stock cube dissolved in 1 pint boiling water
½ tsp English mustard powder
Salt and freshly ground black pepper
300 ml (½ pint) skimmed milk
112g (4 oz) Stilton cheese
2 bay leaves
2 tbspns chopped fresh flat leaf parsley

Remove outer leaves from the cauliflower and coarsely chop the rest. Place in a large saucepan. Add the onions, garlic, vegetable stock, mustard powder and bay leaves. Bring to the boil then reduce the heat and simmer gently for 15 – 20 minutes until the vegetables are soft. Allow to cool slightly, then liquidise. Add milk and Stilton cheese until smooth. Return the soup to the pan and season with salt and black pepper. Adjust the consistency with a little extra milk if required. Garnish with finely chopped parsley and serve immediately.

MARIE'S TOP TIP
√ Medium fat grated mature cheese could be an alternative to Stilton.

Salad Selection

Any of the following make a filling packed lunch. Also, ideal for picnics, B.B.Qs and buffets.

Pasta & Ham Salad

Mix 140g (5oz) cooked whole-wheat pasta with 56g (2oz) diced, lean ham, 56g (2oz) pineapple canned in own juice, 1 tblspn peas and sweetcorn, spring onions, diced red and green pepper, cucumber with 2 tblspns extra light mayonnaise and season to taste. Serve on a bed of shredded lettuce and cherry tomatoes.

Pasta & Tuna Salad

Mix 140g (5oz) cooked whole-wheat pasta with small can tuna in brine, diced pepper, cucumber, grated onion and 2 tblspns sweetcorn with dash lemon juice, black pepper and 2 tblspns extra light mayonnaise, serve with rocket, cherry tomatoes and olives.

Potato & Crispy Bacon Salad

Halve 140g (5oz) of cooked baby new potatoes in skins. Chop 2 grilled rashers of lean back bacon and spring onions. Mix together with 2 tblspns extra light mayonnaise or salad dressing. Serve with shredded lettuce, sliced beefsteak tomato, peppers, celery etc.

Chicken & Pasta Salad

Mix 56g (2oz) cooked chicken with 168g (6oz) cooked whole-wheat pasta, chopped apple with skin, red pepper and spring onion. Stir in 2 tbspns extra light mayo or low fat salad dressing and season to taste. Serve with lots of green salad.

Slimtone's Greek Salad

Shred iceberg lettuce into salad bowl and layer with the following – cubed cucumber, sliced celery, radish, pepper and onion, grated carrot and cress. Top with sliced cherry tomatoes, 56g (2oz) feta cheese and a few green or black olives. Drizzle with balsamic vinegar. Serve with 56g (2oz) French bread.

Salad Daze

Prepare a salad from your vegetable basket and serve with one selection from 'a' and 'b' below:

a. 112g (4oz) cooked chicken or 84g (3oz) lean cooked ham / pork / beef or 112g (4oz) tuna / salmon steak.

b. 168g (6oz) boiled / jacket potato or sweet potato or 140g (5oz) cooked wholemeal pasta / brown rice.

Traditional Main Meals

Now you can enjoy a taste of tradition without worrying about your waistline. The following suggestions include meals for one or all the family and our "Sunday Roast".

Meat - Meals for One (approx. 300 cals)

Chump Chop Dinner

1 lean lamb chop (140g (5oz) raw weight, all visible fat removed) well grilled, 140g (5oz) boiled potatoes, free vegetables from 'Vegetable Basket' serve with Slimtone mint sauce gravy (see page 51).

Roast Lamb, Pork or Beef Dinner

84g (3oz) lamb, pork or beef served with 140g (5oz) boiled potatoes, 1 individual frozen Yorkshire pudding and unlimited vegetables from 'Vegetable Basket'with Slimtone gravy (see page 51). Serve with mint, apple or horseradish sauce as preferred.

Shepherds Pie

Brown 112g (4oz) (raw weight) extra lean minced beef or lamb in a non stick pan, drain off all fat, add chopped onion, carrot, 1 tblspn tomato puree, pinch of mixed herbs. Make stock with 2 tspns gravy granules and ¼ pint of water, cover and simmer for 15 mins. Spoon meat mixture into a small ovenproof dish and top with 140g (5oz) cooked mashed potato. Pop under grill until crisp and brown. Serve with free vegetables from the 'Vegetable Basket'. This recipe is also tasty when the meat is substituted for Quorn or lentils.

MARIE'S TOP TIP

√ Add curry or chilli powder to basic mince recipe for a quick chilli, Bolognese or curry sauce. Serve with 140g (5oz) cooked rice or pasta.

√ For a tasty topping add 1 small sliced leek to potatoes

Fillet Steak with Roasted Vegetables

Mist 140g (5oz) steak with low fat cooking spray and season. Place on health grill and cook to suit taste. Mist a selection of vegetables i.e. butternut squash, cherry tomatoes, mushrooms, peppers, onions and courgettes with low fat spray and seasoning, roast in oven or cook in health grill. Serve with 140g (5oz) jacket or Slimtone 'fried' potatoes.

MARIE'S TOP TIP

√ Mixing 2 tblspns low fat crème fraiche with 1 tspn wholegrain mustard makes a tasty sauce.

Gammon

One 98g (3½ oz) gammon steak, grilled and served with 112g (4 oz) pineapple (in own juice), 140g (5oz) boiled potatoes or Slimtone 'fried' potatoes and lots of free vegetables.

Liver Casserole

Slice small onion and carrot. Place in casserole dish with 112g (4oz) liver, 1 small can chopped tomatoes, 1 level tblspn gravy granules made up with 150ml (4 fl oz) water and 1 level tspn sage & onion stuffing mix. Cover and cook at 180°C/350°F/Gas Mark 4 for 45 mins. Serve with 112g (4oz) boiled potatoes and unlimited selection from 'Vegetable Basket'.

Mushroom & Ham Tagliatelle

Boil and drain 56g (2oz) (dry weight) tagliatelle. Poach chopped mushrooms in water, drain and return to pan with 84g (3oz) low fat soft cheese and 1 tblspn skimmed milk. Gently melt cheese. Stir in 28g (1oz) finely diced wafer thin ham and season with black pepper. Pour over tagliatelle. Sprinkle with 1 tspn grated parmesan cheese (optional) and serve with a selection of salad from 'Vegetable Basket'.

MARIE'S TOP TIP

√ One of my favourite quick meals is to cook the tagliatelle. Melt 84g (3oz) low fat soft cream cheese in the microwave. Add 112g (4oz) cooked mixed veg and chopped ham, spoon over tagliatelle and enjoy.

Stir-Fry

Stir-fry selection of vegetables from 'Vegetable Basket' in stock cube, add 112g (4oz) cooked prawns, chicken, quorn or 84g (3oz) pork with 1 tblspn of soy sauce until heated through. Serve with 168g (6oz) cooked rice/pasta and Slimtone curry sauce (see page 51).

MARIE'S TOP TIP

√ For convenience this can be substituted by 1 packet of supermarket ready prepared stir-fry vegetables.

Boiled Ham & Parsley Sauce

84g (3oz) cooked lean boiled ham. Serve with 140g (5oz) boiled potatoes, unlimited vegetables from 'Vegetable Basket' and Slimtone parsley sauce (see page 51).

Family Meals

Bangers & Mash with Tomato & Onion Gravy

Serves 4 – approx 300 cals – 9g fat per serving

Grill 8 thick low fat pork / Quorn sausages. Cook 454g (1 lb) potatoes and mash with ¼ pt skimmed milk. To make gravy place 1 chopped onion, 56g (2oz) mushrooms, 1 tin tomatoes and pinch of mixed herbs in pan and cook gently for 5 mins. Dissolve a beef stock cube in a little water and add to gravy. Simmer for 2 mins and serve with sausage, potatoes and lots of free vegetables.

Peppered Beef & Pasta Bake

Serves 4 – approx 350 cals - 10g fat per serving

140g (5oz) pasta (dry weight), any variety
☺ whole wheat
336g (12oz) extra lean minced beef/chicken etc
112g (4oz) onion, chopped
112g (4oz) peppers, chopped
140g (5oz) mushrooms, sliced
1 can chopped tomatoes
1 tblspn tomato puree

Chopped parsley to garnish
Salt and black pepper

Dry-fry the minced beef in a large non-stick pan until it is evenly browned. Drain off any excess fat. Add chopped tomatoes and tomato puree, mushrooms, peppers, onions and seasonings and cook for a few minutes. Meanwhile, boil the pasta in lightly salted water until tender. Drain and mix pasta with sauce. Serve with green vegetables and lots of salad.

Alternatively, transfer to an oven-proof dish, sprinkle over 56g (2oz) half fat grated cheese and bake for 30 minutes at 200°C/400°F/Gas Mark 6 until cheese is lightly golden. Sprinkle with the parsley and serve. (approx 390 cals/12 g fat).

MARIE'S TOP TIP

✓ I always add sliced courgettes to main recipe. Several members prefer to use rice instead of pasta.

Spaghetti Bolognese

Serves 2 – approx 400 cals - 6.1g fat per serving

224 g (8 oz) extra lean minced beef
56g (2 oz) carrots
112g (4 oz) spaghetti (dry weight)
☺ whole wheat spaghetti
1 small tomato
56g (2 oz) mushrooms
1 tin chopped tomatoes
1 tblspn tomato puree
Fresh parsley sprigs

Brown the mince beef in a non-stick pan and then drain off all the fat. Slice the mushrooms, dice the carrots and add to the meat with chopped tomatoes and tomato puree. Bring to the boil, cover and simmer for 20 minutes. Boil the spaghetti until just tender and top with the sauce. Garnish with tomato and parsley.

Hearty Beef and Beer Casserole

Serves 4 – approx 195 calories - 3.5g fat per serving

392g (14oz) lean stewing steak, cubed
2 onions, finely chopped
2 tblspns plain flour
2 carrots, sliced
4 sticks celery, sliced
196g (7oz) baby button mushrooms
300ml beef stock
¼ pint beer (could use Guinness – rich in iron!)
Salt and black pepper

Preheat the oven to 150°C/200°F/Gas Mark 2. Spray a non stick casserole dish with low fat cooking spray. Season the beef and fry on a high heat, add the onions and stir fry for approx 5 minutes. Add the flour and stir to coat the meat. Add the carrots, celery and mushrooms and stir fry together for a couple of minutes taking care not to let the flour burn. Pour over the stock and beer and stir. Cover and place in the oven for 1 hour, stirring occasionally.

Oriental Pork

Serves 4 – approx 259 cals – 10.6g fat per serving

450g (1 lb) lean pork
1 x 196g (7oz) can pineapple in natural juice
28g (1oz) flour
1 tblspn oil
☺ sesame oil is oriental and rich in healthy fats
565g (1 ¼ lb) potatoes, cubed
1 tspn Five Spice seasoning
¾ pint (450 ml) beef stock
3 large carrots, sliced
1 large onion, sliced
Black pepper
2 tblspns soy sauce

Cut pork into narrow strips, place in plastic bag with flour, Five Spice seasoning and black pepper. Shake bag until meat is well coated. Heat oil, fry meat until sealed. Add onions, carrots, soy sauce, beef stock, potatoes, pineapples and juice. Simmer for 30-35 mins or until vegetables and meat are cooked throughout.

Pork Surprise

Serves 4 – approx 250 cals – 7.4g fat per serving

4 lean pork steaks/chops approx 112g (4oz)
1 onion
2 tspns medium curry powder
2 yellow peppers
275ml (½ pint) chicken stock
1 tblspn plain flour
112g (4oz) dry apricots (ready to eat/no soak)
2 tblspn wholegrain mustard

Dry fry pork steaks to seal and place in casserole dish. Mix curry powder, flour and mustard to a paste and spread over steaks. Dry fry chopped onions and peppers until soft. Spoon over steaks. Cook slowly for approx 45 mins or until meat is cooked. Add apricots, return to the oven and cook for a further 15 mins.

Poultry - Meals for One (approx. 300 cals)

Roast Chicken Dinner

112g (4oz) roast chicken or turkey (no skin), served with 140g (5oz) boiled/Slimtone roast potatoes, 84g (3oz) peas or broad beans and unlimited vegetables from 'Vegetable Basket' with Slimtone sage & onion flavoured gravy (see page 51).

Chicken Casserole

Place 1 boneless chicken breast (approx. 112g (4oz) no skin) in an ovenproof dish, add 1 small can chopped tomatoes with herbs, small sliced onion, diced carrots and sliced mushrooms and seasoning. Cook in microwave for 8 mins or 180°C/350°F/Gas Mark 4 for 35 mins. (Half a packet of chasseur/casserole mix can be substituted for tomatoes if preferred). Serve with unlimited vegetables from 'Vegetable Basket' and 140g (5oz) mashed/boiled potatoes.

Creamy Chicken Pasta

Add a pinch of salt and mixed herbs to a saucepan of water and cook 56g (2oz) dry pasta according to instructions. Spray non-stick frying pan and cook 112g (4oz) diced skinless chicken pieces with garlic to taste. Fold in 2 tblspn half fat crème fraiche, mixed herbs and simmer. Season to taste. Drain pasta, and toss in the chicken mixture. Serve with salad and garnish with parsley.

MARIE'S TOP TIP

√ If sauce seems a bit dry, thin with a little cooking water from pasta.

Chicken Kiev

Split one 112g (4oz) boneless, skinless chicken breast and fill 1 tblspn low fat soft cheese with garlic and herb. Make into a parcel by wrapping with two slices of turkey rashers secured with a wooden cocktail stick. Bake in foil in medium hot oven for approximately 20 mins or until thoroughly cooked. Serve with 140g (5oz) Slimtone 'fried' potatoes and unlimited selection from 'Vegetable Basket'.

Quick Chicken Curry

Sweat 1 sliced onion in ½ a chicken stock cube mixed with 150ml (4 fl oz) water. Add 112g (4oz) cubed chicken or quorn, curry powder to taste and sliced mushrooms. Simmer until thoroughly cooked adding more stock if required. Thicken with 2 tspns of cornflour made into a paste with cold water. Serve with 168g (6oz) cooked rice.

Family Meals

Basque Style Chicken

Serves 2 – approx. 250 cals – 4.2g fat per serving

2 x 112g (4oz) Skinless boneless chicken breast
1 green pepper, sliced
1 onion, chopped
1 tspn oregano
2 tspn artificial sweetener
1 large can chopped tomatoes
1 x 5 fl oz / 140 ml dry white wine
1 clove garlic, crushed
2 tspn cornflour mixed with 2 tblspns water
Salt & ground black pepper

Place tomatoes, oregano, garlic, wine, onion, salt and pepper in a saucepan and bring to the boil. Add the chicken breast and bring back to the boil then reduce heat and cover. Simmer gently with lid on for about 15 mins. Add green pepper, simmer for a further 15 mins until chicken is cooked through, then remove chicken. Stir the cornflour paste into the sauce. Simmer for about 1 min, stirring continuously. Take off heat and stir in the sweetener. Pour sauce over chicken and serve.

Chicken & Mushroom Curry

Serves 4 – 140 calories - 4g fat per portion

450g (1 lb) uncooked diced boneless chicken breast
2 tblspns curry paste
1 medium onion, chopped
2 tblspns curry powder
2 cloves garlic, crushed
336g (12oz) mushrooms, sliced
1 tblspn flour to thicken
Salt to season
¾ pint stock made with chicken stock cube

In a non-stick pan, dry fry the chicken, onion, garlic and mushrooms for about 5 mins. Once the juices start to flow add the curry powder and paste. Stir well to ensure all the chicken and vegetables are coated with the spices. Cook for 2-3 mins. Add the stock, bring to the boil then turn down the heat, cover and simmer for 35-45 mins (ensure chicken is cooked through). Mix the flour with a little water to form a paste and stir into the curry to thicken. Cook for a further 4-5 mins until thick.

MARIE'S TOP TIP

√ Curry in a Hurry – in a non-stick pan add chicken, onions and mushrooms. Stir in a jar of low fat curry sauce and a ½ cup of water, simmer until cooked.

Fish & Seafood – Meals for One (approx. 300 cals)

Fish 'n' Parsley Sauce
168g (6oz) any white fish (cod, hake, plaice etc) poached, steamed or microwaved. Serve with portion of Slimtone parsley sauce (see page 51), 140g (5oz) potatoes and unlimited vegetables from 'Vegetable Basket'.

Salmon or Tuna Steak
Poach, grill or bake in foil one 112g (4oz) salmon or tuna steak topped with 1 tspn low fat spread and garnished with dill. Serve with 140g (5oz) boiled new potatoes, unlimited salad or vegetables from the 'Vegetable Basket'.

MARIE'S TOP TIP
- √ Fish is delicious cooked in your health grill.
- √ For a tasty dressing I always pop 56g (2oz) low fat cream cheese into the micro for 1 min. Mix with 1 tblspn extra light mayo and drizzle over fish.

Trout or Sea Bass
One 168g (6oz) trout or sea bass fillet, steamed, grilled or microwaved, served with 140g (5oz) boiled or jacket potato, 112g (4oz) peas and unlimited vegetables from 'Vegetable Basket'.

MARIE'S TOP TIP
- √ Sea Bass is delicious served topped with roasted vegetables, tomatoes and olives.

Catch of the Day
168g (6oz) grilled plaice with 2 level tspns low fat spread, 112g (4oz) potatoes and 112g (4oz) frozen peas.

Fish 'n' Fries
4 grilled fish fingers or veggie fingers, 140g (5oz) of Slimtone 'fried' potatoes or 1 small can of baked beans or spaghetti.

Fish Pie
Place 1 cooked 'Cod in Sauce' in a shallow dish. Top with 140g (5oz) cooked pasta or 168g (6oz) mashed potatoes and 28g (1oz) medium fat cheddar cheese grated. Grill and serve with unlimited vegetables from the 'Vegetable Basket'.

Plan 1 ☺G.I.Jumpstart Menu

This week's daily menus are a selection from your G.I. Jumpstart Plan. They provide slow release energy and satisfy your appetite for a longer period of time, preventing those dreaded hunger pangs and make you less inclined to look for quick fix snacks. It can be used at any time you want a quick, safe and permanent weight loss.

	MONDAY	TUESDAY	WEDNESDAY
BREAKFAST 200 CALS	1 thick slice wholemeal bread topped with small tin of baked beans (curry powder can be added to beans for extra flavour).	1oz (28g) porridge oats made up with water and skimmed milk & 1 medium slice granary toast with grilled tomatoes.	Scrambled, boiled or poached egg on 1 sllice of granary toast served with grilled tomatoes.
LIGHT MEAL 300 CALS	2 medium slices granary bread spread with low fat mayonnaise and filled with chopped egg, rocket, and cherry tomatoes.	1 Slimtone toastie made with granary bread (see page 21) or Chicken and Pasta salad (see page 31).	Portion of Slimtone soup served with granary roll followed by 1 small pot low fat rice pudding.
MAIN MEAL/ READY MEALS 300 CALS/12G FAT	Chicken kiev (see page 39) served with 5 ozs (140g) baby new potatoes, lots of green beans and broccoli.	Spaghetti Bolognese (see page 37).	Quick chicken / quorn curry (see page 41) served with 5ozs (140g) cooked basmati / brown rice.
SNACKS OR TREATS 250 CALS	1 oz (28g) wholegrain breakfast cereal topped with strawberries or blueberries and 1 two fingered Kit Kat.	3 wholemeal crackers/ oatcakes/multigrain Ryvita with 2 oz (56g) low fat soft cheese, cherry tomatoes, 1 sliced apple and 1 cup of drinking chocolate made up with 1/4 pint skimmed milk and 1 tspn drinking chocolate.	2 oz (56g) weetabix cake, small portion of fresh fruit salad and sugar free jelly.

...Don't forget to include your Lifestyle Plan daily allowances

THURSDAY	FRIDAY	SATURDAY	SUNDAY
2 Weetabix with milk from allowance , and 1 small banana or 1 tspn sunflower / pumpkin seeds.	1oz (28g) sultana bran with milk from allowance & 1 slice medium granary/ wholemeal toast spread with low fat cheese triangle.	1 slice wholemeal toast spread with 1 tspn peanut butter and topped with mashed banana.	1 wholemeal roll filled with 2 rashers lean & low bacon. Served with grilled tomatoes and mushrooms.
1 wholemeal pitta bread spread with tomato salsa or low fat mayo filled with wafer thin ham and lots of salad or stir fry vegetables followed by 4 ozs (112g) grapes.	1 wholemeal or granary roll spread with tomato salsa, filled with 2 ozs (56g) chicken and lots of salad	Add 6 oz (168g) of cooked wholewheat pasta and can of chopped tomatoes to a portion of Slimtone soup. Season to taste. Portion of strawberries / raspberries and aerosol cream.	Pasta & Tuna salad (see page 31).
Chicken Casserole (see page 39) Serve with 5oz (140g) new potatoes (with skins) and roasted mediterranean vegetables (see page 52).	2 rashers lean & low bacon grilled, 1 poached / scrambled egg, grilled tomatoes and mushrooms, 5ozs (140g) slimtone fried new potatoes & 1 tablespoon brown sauce.	Grilled salmon steak, 5 ozs (140g) baby new potatoes (or sweet potato wedges) served with green vegetables or a large salad.	Traditional Sunday Roast (see page 33).
Portion of leek & potato soup served with thick slice granary bread.	Spread a wholemeal pitta bread with low fat cheese triangle and fill with wafer thin ham. Pop onto health grill until warm and crisp and enjoy with lots of green salad.	1 packet low fat crisps with 3 vodka & diet coke or 1/2 pint lager or 1 glass of wine.	Portion of fresh fruit salad topped with low fat yoghurt / fromage frais.

Plan 2 - Lifestyle Menu

This week's plan is packed with healthy, great tasting dishes. They can be mixed 'n' matched to suit your lifestyle.

	MONDAY	TUESDAY	WEDNESDAY	
BREAKFAST 200 CALS	2 slices granary toast topped with 1 can of chopped tomatoes flavoured with a dash of worcester sauce and seasoned with black pepper.	1 oz (28g) of your favourite wholegrain cereal or porridge topped with blueberries/ strawberries/ raspberries and low fat yoghurt.	Slice of granary toast topped with cream cheese and mushrooms (Cook 2oz (56g) of low fat cream cheese with garlic and sliced mushrooms on high in micro for 2 mins) serve with grilled tomatoes.	
LIGHT MEAL 300 CALS	Portion of Slimtone Soup and Potato & Crispy Bacon salad (see page 31)	Corned beef and onion jacket (see page 24). Serve with large salad and Slimtone coleslaw.	Granary roll spread with low fat mayo or tomato sauce. Filled with two fish/vegetable fingers and lots of crispy salad or one pre-packed sandwich up to 300 cals and no more than 12g of fat.	
MAIN MEAL/ READY MEALS 300 CALS/12G FAT	Slimtone Quick Chicken Curry (see page 41). Serve with 6 oz (168g) basmati rice	5 oz (140g) grilled steak served with 5 oz (140g) Slimtone fried potatoes, grilled mushrooms and large green salad.	Corned beef gravy (see page 23). Serve with 140g (5oz) boiled potatoes and 'free' veg from 'vegetable basket'.	
SNACKS OR TREATS 250 CALS	Two toasted crumpets spread with low sugar jam served with one low cal drinking chocolate.	Three multigrain ryvita spread with low fat cheese triangle, serve with cherry tomatoes, rocket and one packet of low fat crisps.	3 cream crackers, 1 pick 'n' mix cheese, 1 tblspn sweet pickle served with cherry tomatoes	

THURSDAY	FRIDAY	SATURDAY	SUNDAY
Toast 1 thick slice granary bread, top with 4 oz (112g) plain cottage cheese. Pop under grill and serve with grilled tomatoes and mushrooms.	TAKE TWO: 1 oz of your favourite breakfast cereal with milk from allowance & 1 medium slice of toast with low fat cheese triangle & grilled tomatoes.	Make up 1½ oz (42g) porridge oats with water and top with 3 oz (84g) strawberries/raspberries or fruit compote.	Grill 3 turkey rashers, serve with poached/scrambled egg, grilled tomatoes, Slimtone garlic mushrooms and one thin slice of toast.
Chicken and pasta salad (see page 31)	1 serving of Ham & Pea Soup (see page 27) and a slice of wholemeal bread or 5 ozs (140g) boiled new potatoes	One corned beef and onion toastie (see page 24) Serve with green salad or can of chopped tomatoes.	Fill 1 panini with low fat cream cheese, wafer thin ham and sliced spring onions. Heat in Health Grill and follow with piece of fruit from fruit bowl.
Cook 1 lean lamb chop (5 oz (140g) raw weight). Serve with 5oz (140g) boiled potatoes, lots of free vegetables and Slimtone minted gravy (see page 51)	3 grilled fish fingers or veggie fingers served with 5 oz (140g) Slimtone potato wedges and free veg.	Bangers and Mash with Tomato & Onion Gravy (see page 35) served with colcannon (see page 49)	Traditional Sunday Roast (see page 33)
1 toasted teacake served with 1 tspn of sugar free jam or 2 tspns of low fat spread	2 small slices currant loaf toasted, spread with 2 tspns half fat butter and low sugar jam.	Two glasses of wine/lager and 1 packet of low fat crisps.	Portion of Slimtone Lemon and Lime cheesecake (see page 57) and two fingered Kit Kat.

...Don't forget to include your Lifestyle Plan daily allowances

Plan 3 - Lifestyle Menu

This week's plan is packed with healthy, great tasting dishes. You can replace with your favourite recipes from the Lifestyle Plan: You will notice these have been colour coded for your convenience

	MONDAY	TUESDAY	WEDNESDAY	
BREAKFAST 200 CALS	1 oz (28g) porridge or bran cereals topped with 2 tspns of fruit compote, blueberries/ cranberries and 1 small pot of low fat yoghurt.	1 Weetabix or oatbix with milk from allowance topped with half a small banana. One slice of granary toast spread with remainder of banana.	1oz (28g) of your favourite wholegrain breakfast cereal with milk from allowance & 1 tin grapefruit segments in natural juice or 2 fruits from your Slimtone 'fruit basket'.	
LIGHT MEAL 300 CALS	Egg and bacon jacket potato, snip 2 grilled turkey rashers and mix with cooked potato filling and cherry tomatoes and chives, pop back into potato and top with a poached egg	Make up a Spanish omelette by dry-frying chopped red pepper with a few sliced spring onions. Add 4 boiled sliced potatoes, a little chopped corriander and 2 beaten eggs. Cook until set.	Fill a panini with two thin slices of corned beef and onion. Pop onto health grill and serve with cherry tomatoes, rocket and Slimtone coleslaw.	
MAIN MEAL/ READY MEALS 300 CALS/12G FAT	One cooked salmon steak, served with 5ozs (140g) new potatoes (with skins), lots of green salad and 1 tblspn of low fat mayo or try our fish Pie (see page 43)	Portion of our Chicken Casserole (see page 39) with 5oz (140g) mashed potatoes and unlimited free vegetables.	Portion of Slimtone chicken & mushroom curry (see page 41) served with 6oz (168g) cooked basmati/brown rice.	
SNACKS OR TREATS 250 CALS	1 pot of low fat fromage frais and 3 selections from your fruit basket	Three multigrain ryvita spread with low fat cheese triangle, wafer thin ham and sliced tomatoes. Serve with sliced apple and 3½oz (98g) grapes.	Portion of broccoli soup (see page 27) served with a small granary roll.	

THURSDAY	FRIDAY	SATURDAY	SUNDAY
1 slice thick granary toast topped with 2 turkey rashers. Serve with grilled mushrooms, cherry tomatoes, poached/ scrambled egg and 1 tblspn brown sauce.	1 thick slice of toast topped with banana or small can baked beans.	Halve a wholemeal muffin. Toast and sandwich together with 1 small poached egg and 1oz (28g) wafer thin ham.	Two grilled thin low fat sausages and large tomato served on a thick slice of granary bread.
Dice 2oz (56g) lean cooked chicken. Mix with curry paste and portion of Slimtone coleslaw and spoon over one 8oz cooked jacket potato. Or into a wholemeal pitta bread. Serve with lots of salad.	Spread 2 medium slices of granary bread with low fat cream cheese flavoured with onion & chive, fill with wafer thin ham. Serve with salad (This makes a tasty toastie).	Portion of ham & pea soup (see page 27) served with 5oz (140g) baby new potatoes	2 slices wholemeal bread/medium bap or crusty roll filled with 1 tbspn low fat mayonnaise, one small can of tuna, shredded lettuce, cucumber and rocket.
One grilled gammon steak (fat removed) topped with sliced pineapple, served with 5oz (140g) Slimtone fried potatoes or sweet potato wedges grilled tomatoes and mushrooms.	Portion of Slimtone shepherds pie (see page 33) served with lots of free vegetables.	Fillet steak with roasted vegetables (see page 33) served with 5oz (140g) jacket or Slimtone fried potatoes	3 oz (84g) roast beef served with 5 oz (140g) boiled potatoes, 1 individual frozen yorkshire pudding, unlimited free vegetables and Slimtone gravy.
2 toasted crumpets topped with tspn sugar free jam served with low cal drinking chocolate.	One mug of drinking chocolate made with skimmed milk and 2 level tbspns cocoa powder, 2 rich tea biscuits.	½ Bottle (approx 3 glasses) of red or white wine	Portion of Slimtone steam pudding (see page 57) served with low fat custard.

...Don't forget to include your Lifestyle Plan daily allowances

Plan 4 - Lifestyle Menu

This week's plan is packed with healthy, great tasting dishes. You can replace with your favourite recipes from the Lifestyle Plan.

	MONDAY	TUESDAY	WEDNESDAY
BREAKFAST 200 CALS	1oz (28g) porridge oats topped with a small diced banana or 1oz (28g) raisins made up with milk from allowance.	Toast thick slice of wholemeal bread and top with 1 well grilled back bacon rasher, grilled mushrooms and tomatoes.	Toast 2 medium slices of wholemeal/granary bread spread with 2oz (56g) low fat cream cheese, topped with grilled tomatoes.
LIGHT MEAL 300 CALS	6oz (168g) cooked pasta mixed with small can drained tuna in brine, chopped spring onions, cucumber, cherry tomatoes and two tblspn low fat mayo.	Spread 1 bread wrap with low fat mayo/ salsa and fill with 3oz (84g) chicken and lots of crispy lettuce.	Bake an 8oz (224g) jacket potato and top with large portion of Slimtone coleslaw mixed with 1oz (28g) grated medium fat cheddar cheese or 1oz (28g) prawns. Serve with a large salad.
MAIN MEAL/ READY MEALS 300 CALS/12G FAT	Corned beef casserole (see page 23). Serve with lots of free vegetables.	Grill 2 cod fish cakes/4 fish or veggie fingers. Serve with 5oz (140g) Slimtone 'fried' potatoes or wedges, 3 tblspns peas and large salad.	Shepherds Pie (see page 33)
SNACKS OR TREATS 250 CALS	2 toasted crumpets with 2 tspns each of low-fat spread and jam. Plus 1 kiwi fruit.	1 serving of Slimtone Super Soup (see page 30) and 1 thin slice wholemeal bread.	1 medium finger roll with 1 jumbo tinned hot dog, poached onions and ketchup.

THURSDAY	FRIDAY	SATURDAY	SUNDAY
1½oz (42g) porridge oats cooked in water and served with milk from allowance topped with sliced strawberries/blueberries and 1 small pot fruit of the forest yoghurt.	TAKE TWO: 1 Weetabix with ½ medium banana and milk from allowance & 1 thick slice wholemeal toast spread with remainder of banana.	Grill 3 turkey rashers. Serve with 1 poached egg, grilled tomatoes, Slimtone garlic mushrooms and 1 thin slice wholemeal toast.	4oz (112g) seedless grapes and 4oz (112g) chopped melon topped with 1oz (28g) museli and 1 pot of low fat yoghurt/fromage frais.
Fritata/omelette made with 2 eggs filled with cooked chopped vegetables and one small cubed cooked potato.	Toast 1 thick slice of wholemeal bread and top with 4oz (112g) of sardines canned in tomato sauce. Serve with a selection of green salad.	1 panini filled with low fat cream cheese, wafer thin ham, pop on to a health grill. Enjoy with green salad.	Portion of Slimtone Soup followed by - 3oz (84g) chunk of french bread with 1oz (28g) brie/low fat cheddar cheese, 3oz (84g) grapes and a large salad.
Portion of corned beef gravy (see page 23) served with 5oz (140g) boiled potatoes and lots of free vegetables.	One portion of curry in a hurry (see page 41) served with 6oz (168g) cooked basmati rice.	4oz (112g) salmon cooked in foil with spring onions and lemon juice, served with 5oz (140g) new/sweet potatoes, mediterranean roasted vegetables (see page 52)	Traditional Sunday Roast (see page 33) and sugar free jelly served with 1 tbspn Aerosol cream.
3 Wholemeal crackers with 2oz (56g) low fat soft cheese, salad, 1 apple and 3oz (84g) grapes.	1 salad roll and 1 packet of low fat crisps.	2 glasses of wine/lager with 1 packet low fat crisps.	2 thick slices toast topped with 1 poached egg.

...Don't forget to include your Lifestyle Plan daily allowances

Plan 5 - Lifestyle Quick 'n' Easy Menu

This week's menu will provide tasty, easy to make meals when in a hurry. Don't forget to take a look at our Easy Meals for Busy Days in your Lifestyle Plan.

	MONDAY	TUESDAY	WEDNESDAY
BREAKFAST 200 CALS	1oz (28g) porridge or bran cereals topped with 2 tspns of fruit compote, blueberries and 1 diet yoghurt	Small glass fresh orange juice and 1 thick slice toast topped with scrambled/poached/boiled egg and grilled tomato.	1oz (28g) porridge oats made with water and served with milk from allowance. 1 medium slice wholemeal toast with grilled or tinned tomatoes.
LIGHT MEAL 300 CALS	Egg and bacon jacket potato, snip 1 slice cooked lean back bacon, mix with cooked potato filling and cherry tomatoes and chives, pop back into potato and top with a poached egg.	Portion of Slimtone soup, with 5oz (140g) cooked pasta shells, 1 can chopped tomatoes, pinch of mixed herbs. Serve with small slice of french bread.	Slimtone toastie (see page 21)
MAIN MEAL/ READY MEALS 300 CALS/12G FAT	Corned beef gravy (see page 23), mash 5oz (140g) potatoes with swede and serve with lots of 'free' vegetables.	2 low fat grilled sausages, portion of colcannon (see page 49). Serve with free veg and portion of Slimtone onion gravy.	4 grilled fish fingers, 5oz (140g) Slimtone fried potatoes, and lots of salad.
SNACKS OR TREATS 250 CALS	1 toasted teacake served with 1 tspn of sugar free jam or 2 tspn of low fat spread.	1 packet low fat crisps served with a dip of 2oz (56g) low fat cream cheese, cherry tomatoes, celery, rocket etc and 1 small glass of red/white wine.	3 cream crackers, 1 pick 'n' mix cheese, 1 tblspn sweet pickle served with cherry tomatoes etc.

THURSDAY	FRIDAY	SATURDAY	SUNDAY
1 thick slice granary bread toasted topped with 5oz (140g) baked beans. * For a different flavour why not add a pinch of curry powder to your baked beans.	1 weetabix served with milk from allowance and half a banana + 1 medium slice granary toast topped with remaining half of banana.	Fill 1 breakfast roll with 2 grilled bacon medalions and 1 tblspn brown sauce.	3 grilled turkey rashers, served with 1 poached egg, grilled tomatoes, Slimtone garlic mushrooms and 1 thin slice of toast.
Panini filled with low fat soft cream cheese and wafer thin ham. Pop onto health grill and enjoy with cherry tomatoes and green salad.	Bread wrap filled with a raita of low fat mayo, mint sauce, corriander, spring onion, natural yoghurt and 2oz (56g) tandori chicken pieces.	Savoury Omelette - Beat together 2 eggs and make an omelette in non stick pan misted with low fat cooking spray fill with stir fry veg and serve with 5oz (140g) Slimtone fried potatoes.	Hot Bacon & Cheese Bagel. Grill 1 rasher of lean bacon and tear into small pieces, cut 2 cheese triangles and divide between the bagels, add bacon & cherry tomatoes, grill for 5 mins.
Corned beef casserole (see page 23)	Shepherd's Pie (see page 33)	Mushroom & Ham Tagliatelle (see page 34) OR your favourite meal from your Lifestyle Plan.	Roast Chicken Dinner (see page 39)
2 small slices currant loaf toasted, spread with low fat cream cheese and reduced sugar jam.	Split 1 white soft roll and sandwich together with 1 pkt of low-fat crisps.	½ Bottle (approx 3 glasses) Red or White wine.	Two Slimtone Welsh cakes (see page 59) and packet of low fat crisps.

...Don't forget to include your Lifestyle Plan daily allowances

Plan 6 - Lifestyle Vegetarian Menu

This week's plan has been designed for vegetarians. However you will see a large selection of tasty meals in the Lifestyle Plan to suit every taste.

	MONDAY	TUESDAY	WEDNESDAY
BREAKFAST 200 CALS	Cook 1oz (28g) porridge oats with 3 dried apricots and top with 1 low fat yoghurt.	2 Weetabix with ¼ pint skimmed milk, topped with sliced strawberries or blueberries.	1oz (28g) porridge topped with sliced strawberries, 1 tspn pumpkin seeds, and 2 tblspns low fat natural yoghurt.
LIGHT MEAL 300 CALS	Mexican omelette (see page 45) served with 5oz (140g) Slimtone fried potatoes and lots of green salad.	Vegetable Omelette made with 2 eggs, filled with 5oz (140g) cooked chopped potatoes, onions, mushrooms, peppers, broccoli etc.	Bake an 8oz (224g) jacket/sweet potato and top with 4oz (112g) cottage cheese and sliced beetroot (optional) or small can of baked beans. Serve with a large salad.
MAIN MEAL/ READY MEALS 300 CALS/12G FAT	2 veggie burgers (see page 47) and large portion of stir fry.	Lasagne (see page 46).	2 Quorn sausages served with Cauliflower Cheese (see page 45)
SNACKS OR TREATS 250 CALS	1 thick slice soya & linseed toast topped with 1 poached egg with 1 peach or nectarine.	2 toasted crumpets or wholemeal muffin with 2 tspns each of low-fat spread and no added sugar jam.	Half a mango, handful of cherries and an apple.

THURSDAY	FRIDAY	SATURDAY	SUNDAY
1oz (28g) of your favourite wholegrain breakfast cereal topped with a small sliced banana or 1oz (28g) raisins and serve with milk from allowance.	1 thick slice of wholemeal/granary/ soya & linseed toast topped with small can of baked beans.	Toast 1 thick slice of wholemeal bread and serve with 2 tspns low-fat spread and 1 medium poached egg, grilled or canned tomatoes and mushrooms.	2 slices wholemeal toast with 1 can chopped tomatoes with a dash of worcester sauce, tomato puree, black pepper & basil.
Spread 1 bread wrap/ wholemeal pitta with extra light mayo/salsa and fill with stir fry vegetables and one small banana.	Split one wholemeal bap/pitta. Spread with tomato puree, top with 1oz (28g) grated cheese, chopped spring onion, sliced mushrooms and tomato. Season with oregano. Grill and serve with salad.	1 panini filled with low fat cream cheese, sliced tomatoes and red onions, pop onto health grill and enjoy with mixed salad.	Serve 3oz (84g) chunk of french bread with 1oz (28g) cheese, 3oz (84g) grapes, celery, cherry tomatoes and a large salad.
Cauliflower & broccoli bake (see page 45)	Sweet & Sour Stir Fry (see page 46)	Vegetable Curry (see page 46).	2 vegetarian/Quorn sausages, 1 frozen Ind Yorkshire Pudding. 5oz (140g) boiled potatoes, lots of free vegetables, served with fat free gravy.
3 Wholemeal crackers/ oatcakes/multigrain ryvita with 2oz (56g) low-fat soft cheese, salad, 1 apple and 3oz (84g) grapes.	1 sliced banana served with small pot of low fat custard.	2 glasses of red wine or 2 glasses of lager with 1 packet low fat crisps.	Slice of berry & banana tart (see page 55) and an individual low fat rice pudding..

...Don't forget to include your Lifestyle Plan daily allowances

Steamed Sea Bass with Chilli

Season a 140g (5oz) Sea Bass steak with salt and black pepper and place in top of a steamer. Sprinkle over sliced spring onions, chopped ginger, garlic and chilli. Pour 1 tspn of lime juice over the fish. Steam the fish gently for 5 minutes. Serve with 168g (6oz) Slimtone potato wedges and green salad.

Haddock

Lightly poach 224g (8oz) haddock and serve with mixed salad and 140g (5oz) boiled potatoes or 1 medium slice wholemeal bread and 2 tspns low fat spread.

Tuna & Tarragon Pasta

Cook 56 g (2oz) (uncooked weight) of pasta as directed. Meanwhile drain and flake 1 small can of tuna in brine, mix with 1 tbspn chopped tarragon, 1 tbspn tarragon vinegar and 1 tbspn tomato ketchup. Place the mixture into a saucepan. Add 56g (2oz) of frozen peas or petit pois and 56g (2oz) drained canned sweetcorn. Mix well and heat thoroughly. Drain the pasta and top with the tuna sauce. Season to taste with freshly ground black pepper.

Family Meals
Salmon and Pasta Bake

Serves 4 – approx. 274 cals – 9.3 g fat per serving

56g (2oz) grated half fat cheddar cheese
210g (7 ½ oz) can red salmon, drained
336g (12 oz) cooked pasta (115g (4oz) dry weight)
☺ whole wheat pasta
112g (4oz) sliced courgettes
112g (4oz) sliced mushrooms
84g (3oz) sliced onions

Sauce
2 level tspn (10 ml) cornflour
¾ pint (450 ml) skimmed milk
1 vegetable stock cube

Place onions, mushrooms, courgettes in a non-stick pan and sauté for 4-5 mins until soft. Break the salmon into bite sized pieces and divide between 4 heatproof dishes, add pasta and vegetables. Mix cornflour with a little milk. Heat remaining milk with stock cube in a pan and pour into cornflour, stirring continuously until thickened. Pour into dishes, sprinkle over grated cheese and grill until melted.

Pan-Fried Sole with Tomato Pesto
Serves 4 – approx 300 cals – 4.5 g fat per serving

To make the pesto, place 224g (8oz) sundried tomatoes in a saucepan and cover with water. Heat until boiling, then simmer for 10 minutes until soft. Once cool, pour into a food processor, add 1 tbspn chopped coriander and process until smooth, adding more water to achieve a sauce-like consistency.

Spray a griddle pan with low fat spray. Season 4 fillets of Dover sole on both sides and cook over a high heat for 2-3 mins on each side. Transfer the fish to a serving dish and spoon over the pesto. Serve with 140g (5oz) baby new potatoes in their skins, broccoli and green beans.

MARIE'S TOP TIP

√ For convenience the ready prepared pesto available in all supermarkets is ideal for this recipe.

Vegetarian – Meals for One (approx. 300 cals)

Cauliflower and Broccoli Bake
Place cooked cauliflower and broccoli florets in an ovenproof dish, spoon over 140g (5oz) cooked pasta. Make up a portion of Slimtone cheese sauce (see page 51). Pour over pasta and grill until golden. Serve with lots of green salad.

Sliced Sausage and Cauliflower Cheese
Lightly cook cauliflower and place in a shallow heat-proof dish. Make up cheese sauce with ¼ pint skimmed milk, 2 tspns cornflour and 28g (1oz) grated medium fat cheddar cheese (full flavour). Spoon over cauliflower. Serve with 2 sliced Quorn sausages plus cherry tomatoes and mushrooms.

MARIE'S TOP TIP

√ Broccoli added to cauliflower when cooking is a tasty addition to this dish.

Mexican Omelette
Make up omelette in non-stick pan with 2 medium-sized eggs. Fill with mushrooms, vine ripened tomatoes, peppers, spring onions, etc. Slide onto warm plate and serve with 140g (5oz) baby new potatoes.

MARIE'S TOP TIP

√ Pop potatoes on baking tray, mist with low cal cooking spray and bake in hot oven until crisp and brown. A tasty alternative to chips....

Tasty Waffles

Top 2 Potato Waffles with one of the following:
a. 1 medium-sized poached or scrambled egg.
b. 1 small can of baked beans or spaghetti.
c. 1 well-grilled low fat vegeburger

Serve with grilled tomatoes, Slimtone garlic mushrooms and salad.

MARIE'S TOP TIP

√   Pop waffles into toaster to heat.

Vegetable Curry

Mist pan with cooking spray. Sauté 1 chopped onion and 56g (2oz) mushrooms until tender. Add curry power and cook for 2 mins, stirring continuously. Add 112g (4oz) tinned tomatoes and 168g (6oz) fresh or frozen mixed vegetables with just enough water to cover. Simmer until tender and serve with 168g (6oz) cooked rice and 1 tblspn mango chutney.

MARIE'S TOP TIP

√   Make up a delicious Raita simply by mixing 2 tblspns natural yoghurt, garlic and mint.

Sweet & Sour Stir Fry Quorn

Make up marinade with 1 tblspn of soy sauce, 1 tblspn orange juice and 1 tblspn water, 1 tspn tomato puree, 1 tspn wine vinegar, 1 tspn sugar and ½ tspn cornflour. Leave 56g (2oz) Quorn cubes in marinade for at least 1hour. Stir fry 2 chopped spring onions, ½ chopped chilli and 1 tspn grated fresh ginger in 1 tspn oil. Add selection of free vegetables. Cook for 2 mins. Add Quorn and marinade liquid and cook for 2-3 mins. Serve with 168g (6oz) cooked rice (2oz dry weight).

Vegetable Lasagne

Sauté 1 tblspn of chopped onion and garlic in 1 tspn oil to soften. Add 56g (2oz) minced Quorn, ½ chopped green pepper and small can tomatoes. Simmer for 15 mins. Mix 1 small courgette with 56g (2oz) low fat soft cheese. Mist dish with low fat cooking spray, add layers of tomato sauce, courgettes and cheese between 2 fresh lasagne sheets – finish with tomato sauce. Cover with foil and bake for 45 mins, 190°C/375°F/ Gas 5. Sprinkle with 2 tspns of grated parmesan cheese and serve.

Family Meals

Vegetarian Burgers

Serves 4 - 126 cals - 3.8g fat per serving

Cook 112 g (4oz) chopped mushrooms in a non-stick pan without oil, stirring, for 8-10 minutes to drive off all the moisture. Process 1 onion, 1 small courgette, 1 carrot and 25g (1oz) unsalted peanuts / cashew nuts in a food processor until the ingredients begin to bind together. Stir in the mushrooms, 112g (4oz) breadcrumbs, 2 tblspns chopped fresh parsley, 1 tblspn yeast extract and season with salt & pepper to taste. Shape into four burgers and then chill. Cook the burgers in a non-stick frying pan, or under a hot grill for 8-10 minutes, turning once, until the burgers are cooked and golden brown. Serve hot with a crisp salad.

Tofu and Green Bean Curry

Serves 4 - 100 cals- 3.3g fat per serving

350 ml (12 fl oz) coconut milk
1 tspn red curry paste
3 tblspns fish sauce
2 tspns sugar
224g (8oz) button mushrooms
112g (4oz) French green beans, trimmed
174g (6oz) bean curd (tofu), rinsed and cut into 2 cm / ¾ inch cubes
4 kaffir lime leaves, torn
2 red chillies, seeded and sliced
Fresh coriander leaves to garnish

Put about 1/3 of the coconut milk into a wok or saucepan. Cook until it starts to separate and an oily sheen appears. Add the red curry paste, fish sauce and sugar to the coconut milk and mix thoroughly. Add the mushrooms. Stir and cook for 1 minute. Stir in the rest of the coconut milk and bring back to the boil. Add the French beans and tofu, simmer gently for another 4-5 minutes. Stir in the kaffir lime leaves and chillies. Serve garnished with the coriander leaves. Serve with 174g (6oz) cooked rice per portion.

Vegetarians : Please note – All Slimtone recipes and menus can be adapted by substituting Quorn or tofu for meat and poultry. Quorn is extremely low in fat and has a succulent texture and quickly absorbs the flavours of herbs and spices during cooking. Tofu is versatile, adopts flavours well and also has many health benefits including cholesterol lowering and hormonal balancing.

When using convenience ready meals please ensure that these do not exceed 300 calories and 12g fat per serving.

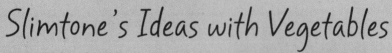

Slimtone's Ideas with Vegetables

Using a selection from your 'Vegetable Basket' the following are ideal as a tasty, low calorie addition to your meals and an ideal way of making the most of your Take '5' Selection.

Slimtone Coleslaw

Mix any of the following with 1 tblspn of low fat salad dressing or extra light mayonnaise: shredded white cabbage, onions, carrots, peppers, cauliflower, celery, cucumber, mushrooms, cress, red cabbage or beansprouts.

Slimtone Vegetable Curry

Mix one 392g (14oz) can of chopped tomatoes with mixed peppers, chopped mushrooms, cauliflower, broccoli, carrots, sweetcorn and 1 curry flavour stock cube. Place all ingredients together in a large non-stick pan and slowly bring to the boil, reduce heat and leave to simmer for 15 mins.

Slimtone Stir-fry

Spray non-stick pan or wok with low-cal spray and cook a selection of "free" vegetables e.g. beansprouts, onions, mushrooms, peppers, carrots, broccoli, cauliflower florets etc. For added flavour try one of the great ranges of stir-fry stock cubes or soy sauce. Makes a great filling for a bread wrap, simply add chopped chicken and drizzle with salsa or sweet chilli sauce.

Roasted Mediterranean Vegetables

Roughly chop a selection of courgette, red onion, mushroom, peppers and aubergine and place on a baking tray. Spray with low calorie cooking spray, season with black pepper & Mediterranean herbs such as basil or oregano. Roast for 20 minutes at 200°C, turning once. Serve drizzled with balsamic vinegar

Savoury Mashed Potatoes

Transform mashed potatoes included in the menus with any of the following:
a. Wholegrain mustard
b. Swede, carrot or leek
c. Tablespoon of pesto and grated Parmesan cheese
d. Colcannon - cook potatoes with sliced green cabbage and spring onions or leeks, season and mash with skimmed milk.

Garlic Mushrooms

Prepare mushrooms and place in an oven-proof dish. Drizzle over garlic sauce or seasoning to taste and cook in microwave for a few minutes.

Slimtone Sauces
& Gravies

The following are a selection of Slimtone favourites
that can add variety to the meals in your Lifestyle Plan.

Slimtone Curry Sauce (95 calories)

Melt 14g (½ oz) low fat spread in a small pan, stir in 1 level tspn of curry powder, cook over a low heat for 2 mins. Add 1 finely chopped onion, ½ pint of water, 2 tblspn tomato chutney and 1 chicken stock cube. Stir and bring to the boil. Cover pan and simmer for 15 mins. Blend 1 level tblspn of cornflour with a little water and add to the pan stirring well. Simmer for 2 mins or until thickened. (Really tasty served with Slimtone fried rice and stir fried vegetables)

Slimtone Gravy

With a little imagination tasty sauces and gravies can be prepared quickly and the following low fat ideas will make a tasty edition to your meal:

For easy, fat free gravy, granules are ideal. Put 2 heaped tspns of granules in a jug and add ¼ pint boiling water (or if available vegetable stock). Alternatively mix 1 heaped tspn of granules and 1 tspn cornflour with a little cold water, add ¼ pint of boiling water or stock.

a. For added flavour add 1 tspn of concentrated mint sauce (20 cals).

b. A tasty gravy can be made by adding 1 tspn of dry stuffing mix e.g. sage & onion, apple & herb, cranberry & orange etc. to the gravy granules and make as above, stir well and microwave for 2 mins to thicken at only 40 calories.

c. For quick savoury gravy simply add sliced cooked onions and a pinch of mixed herbs to granules before making up as directed (20 cals).

Easy Low-Fat White Sauce

Serves 2 – approx 75 cals per portion

Gradually whisk ½ pt skimmed milk into 3 tblspns plain flour. Bring to the boil and cook for 2 mins, stirring until thickened. Season to taste with salt, pepper and 1 tspn vegetable boulion.

MARIE'S TOP TIP

✓ Half a vegetable stock cube can be substituted for boulion.

Variations:

1. Parsley Sauce – add 2 tblspns fresh chopped parsley.

2. Cheese Sauce – add 56g (2oz) low fat cheddar cheese and stir until melted (serves 2 – at 145 per portion)

3. Mushroom Sauce – Add 56g (2oz) sliced mushrooms, poached in 2 tblspns water to basic white sauce.

Low Cal Cooking Spray

Flash in the Pan

One of the most important items you can have in your store cupboard is Low Cal cooking spray. I personally prefer the Olive Oil version, which can be used for any of the Slimtone favourites listed below.

Slimtone "Fried Potatoes"

Thinly slice cooked potatoes, spray with low-cal cooking spray and grill until crisp and brown or spray a non-stick pan and "fry". (Approx 20 cals per ounce)

Sunday "Roasties"

Peel potatoes and place on baking tray, spray with low-cal cooking spray and cook as usual. (Approx 20 cals per 28g (1oz) (I usually par boil my potatoes first)

Parsnips are also great roasted the Slimtone way.

Crisp Jacket Potatoes

Microwave potato as usual (weigh and cook for 1 minute per 28g (1oz). When cooked mist with low-cal spray and pop into a hot oven for 5 minutes until skin is crispy. Alternatively cut into wedges and spray before placing in hot oven. Wedges can be served with salad etc. (Approx 25 cals per 28g (1oz) raw weight).

☺ Try sweet potato wedges.

Slimtone Fried Rice

Spray a non-stick pan and "fry" 140g (5oz) cooked rice, scramble 1 size 3 egg and add to rice, sprinkle over Chinese Five spice seasoning and serve with cooked onions, mushrooms, peppers etc.

Roasted Vegetables

Simply chop a selection of your favourite vegetables e.g. courgettes, peppers, red onion, cherry tomatoes, sweet potato, butternut squash, mushrooms etc. Season with basil, thyme or rosemary. Spray and roast... simple.....

Bubble & Squeak

Mist non-stick pan with low fat cooking spray and 'fry up' selection of 'free' vegetables e.g. cabbage, carrots, brussel sprouts etc.

Slimtone Chips

Scrub potato and chip. Spray grill pan with low fat cooking spray and place chips in pan. Grill until brown, turning frequently to ensure even cooking.

MARIE'S TOP TIP

√ When baking fish spray foil with low-cal spray and season with lemon juice etc before sealing, this will prevent sticking. Great with the fried potatoes and vegetables.

√ I also find the spray useful for "frying" onions, mushrooms, eggs etc.

√ Also, mist dish before scrambling eggs and you will find them easier to serve and the dish easier to wash.

√ Stop your pasta sticking by adding a few sprays when cooking.

Weight Conversions

The following list of conversions will be a useful guideline for recipes etc.

Dry weights

Ounce	Grams
½	14
1	28
1 ½	42
2	56
2 ½	70
3	84
3 ½	98
4	112
4 ½	126
5	140
5 ½	154
6	168
6 ½	182
7	196
7 ½	210
8	224
8 ½	238
9	252
9 ½	266
10	280

Slimtone Puddings & Desserts

With the Lifestyle Plan there's no need to sacrifice life's little pleasures. Slimtone has created low fat, great tasting puddings and desserts, which allow you and your family to enjoy a taste of the sweet life.

Rhubarb Jelly

Serves 4 – Approx. 10 calories per portion

Cover 6-8 sticks of rhubarb with water and simmer gently until cooked. Sprinkle over a packet of raspberry sugar free jelly crystals and leave to set.

Slimtone Fruit Salad

Serves 4 – Approx. 50 calories per portion

Slice a selection of fruit from your 'Fruit Basket' and top with sugar free lemonade or diet apple drink. For a really quick fruit salad why not use one of the frozen fruit selections that are available?

Slimtone Mousse

Serves 4 – Approx. 30 calories per portion

Make up 1 sugar free jelly as directed. When cool divide ½ pint between 4 sundae dishes and leave to set. Stir in 1 low fat yoghurt or fromage frais with remainder and pour over jelly. Chill before serving and top with aerosol cream.

MARIE'S TOP TIP

√ As a quick low calorie trifle, crumble one Weetabix into sundae dishes before following above recipe. Total per trifle – 45 calories

Berry & Banana Tart

Serves 4 – Approx 160 cals - 6g fat per serving

98g (3½oz) ready-prepared sponge flan case
2 large bananas
115g (4oz) reduced-fat crème fraiche
Mint sprigs to decorate (Optional)
6 tblspns orange juice
1 pot low-fat toffee yoghurt
115g (4oz) mixed soft berries such as raspberries and blackberries

Place the flan case on a serving plate and drizzle with the orange juice. Chill for five minutes. Slice the bananas and place in a bowl, reserving half a banana. Carefully fold in the toffee yoghurt and crème fraiche. Spoon the mixture into the prepared sponge case. Scatter the berries over the tart and chill in the fridge for 10 minutes. Decorate the tart with the remaining banana slices and the mint sprigs.

Steam Pudding

Serves 4 – Approx. 150 cals – 3g fat per serving

56g (2oz) self-raising flour (sieved) 2 eggs
56g (2oz) caster sugar
Reduced sugar jam

Mist a 1 pint basin with low fat cooking spray and place 2 tblspn of low sugar jam in the bottom. Warm the mixing bowl. Put in eggs and sugar, beat until mixture is thick and leaves a trail from the whisk. Add flour with a metal spoon. Cover with greaseproof paper, and a layer of foil leaving a pleat for expansion when cooking. Steam for 1 ½ hrs (alternatively, cover loosely with cling film, pierce and cook for approx 3 min in microwave on high – 900w or as per instructions for your microwave). To serve remove cover carefully, run a knife inside of the basin, turn out onto a plate.

Why not serve with a packet of low fat custard, which will serve 4 at approx 75 cals per serving. Total dessert only 225 cals, mmmmm…….

This recipe is most versatile and can be used for a number of desserts i.e. replace 1 tblspn of flour with 1 tblspn cocoa powder for a chocolate pudding. Add the zest of orange or lemon for a citrus flavour.

A delicious dessert can be made with fresh fruit, i.e. apples, blackberries, rhubarb etc. Stew fruit, place in dish and cover with low fat sponge mixture and bake as above.

Lemon & Lime Cheesecake

Serves 8 – approx. 157 cals – 11.1 g fat per serving

7 low fat digestive biscuits, crushed
56g (2oz) low fat spread
1 packet sugar free lemon & lime jelly
2 medium sized eggs (separated)
168g (6oz) low fat cream cheese
140g (5oz) low fat fromage frais

Gently melt low fat spread in a non stick saucepan. Stir in biscuit crumbs and spread in a flan ring. Dissolve sugar free jelly in ¼ pint of hot water and leave to cool. Beat together low fat cream cheese and the 2 egg yolks, add fromage frais and cooled jelly. Whisk egg whites and fold into the mixture. Spread over the biscuit crumbs. Put into fridge to set. Before serving decorate with slices of kiwi, strawberries etc.

MARIE'S TOP TIP

√   This is a favourite dessert with Slimtone members. Any flavour jelly e.g. strawberry/ orange/raspberry can be used.

Low-Fat Welshcakes
Makes 48 – approx. 69 cals – 2 g fat per cake

454g (1 lb) self raising flour   2 medium sized eggs
168g (6oz) sultanas   112g (4oz) caster sugar
196g (7oz) half fat butter

Place flour, butter, sugar and salt in a bowl and rub together until mixture forms breadcrumbs. Add sultanas and mix together with eggs to a rolling consistency. If too dry, add a small amount of water. Roll out to ¼" thick and use a 2 ½" cutter to make 48 cakes. Coat bakestone with low fat cooking spray and cook Welshcakes until golden brown.

Weetabix Cake
approx. 63 cals – 0.4 g fat per 28g (1oz)

2 weetabix
84g (3oz) soft brown sugar
224g (8oz) mixed dried fruits
1 medium egg
224g (8oz) self raising flour
½ pint (300 ml) skimmed milk

Soak weetabix, sugar and fruit in skimmed milk for ½ hour. Gently mix in egg and flour. Place in loaf tin. Bake in oven 180°C/350°F/Gas Mark 4 for approx 1 hour. This can be divided into portions and frozen.

Tropical Brulee
Serves 1 – Approx. 60 calories - neg fat per portion

Place 112g (4oz) of thawed mixed fruits of the forest in a shallow heatproof dish. Spoon over 2 tblspns of 8% fat fromage frais and sprinkle with soft, light brown sugar. Place under a very hot grill for a few mins until the sugar caramelises. Chill before serving.

Slimtone Mince Pies

Makes 40 pies – approx 76 cals each - 2g fat

196g (7oz) mincemeat
196g (7oz) reduced sugar marmalade (mix together)
450g (1 lb) Self raising flour
196g (7oz) half fat butter
Juice and rind of 1 large orange
pinch of salt
Water

Pre-heat oven to 180°C/375°F/Gas Mark 6. Sieve flour and salt into a mixing bowl. Rub in butter until fine breadcrumbs. Add juice and rind of orange with water to make up ½ cup. Mix to a rolling consistency by adding water to mixture. Roll out very thinly on a lightly floured surface making 40 with a 3 inch pastry cutter. Place in patty tins and fill with one tspn (5 ml) of mincemeat mixture. Cut out a further 40 pastry shapes e.g. stars etc and place on top of mincemeat. Place in oven and cook for 12-15 minutes.

Sultana Bread Pudding

Serves 4 – Approx 250cals -6g fat per serving

5 large slices wholemeal bread
84g (3oz) sultanas
28g (1oz) half-fat spread
2 medium eggs
½ tspn grated nutmeg
1 pint skimmed milk

Preheat oven to 180°C/350°F/Gas Mark 4. Spread one side of the bread with the half-fat spread. Cut each slice into four and layer with sugar and sultanas in a 2½-pint ovenproof dish. Whisk the eggs and milk together and pour over the bread. Sprinkle with nutmeg and bake in preheated oven for 45–50 minutes, until the pudding is golden brown and set.

MARIE'S TOP TIP

√ Your Lifestyle Plan gives you an option for daily treats and desserts. It's important that you include these as they are essential in keeping you motivated when losing weight.

√ DON'T FORGET IF YOU BROKE YOUR LEG YOU WOULD NOT THROW AWAY THE CRUTCH.

Slimtone Guide to Eating Out

How to Select the Healthy Option

Losing weight doesn't mean refusing every lunch and dinner invitation, but beware, those menus on offer may be a pleasure for the palate, and a nightmare for the waistline!

When choosing from the menu remember that anything fried, covered in a rich or creamy sauce, mayonnaise, or oil is always high in calories and fat, and so should be avoided. Be aware of portion sizes: many come large enough for two- particularly when eating at Chinese or Indian restaurants. Remember that just because you're paying for it you don't HAVE to eat everything that is in front of you!

Fill your plate with low calorie vegetables, ask that they be served minus a buttery topping. Avoid vegetables that are usually fried e.g. mushrooms, onions, courgettes etc. Salad is a good choice but beware of the dressing and extra toppings such as cheese, bacon and fried onion bits. Always remember the Slimtone rule 'All that glistens is not gold but oil'. Avoid mayonnaise or any coleslaw or potato salad etc. which have a very high fat content or ask if a low calorie alternative is available. If unsure request dressings and sauces to be served on the side.

If you enjoy a glass of white wine with your meal make it into a 'spritzer' by mixing it with soda. If your preference is red wine this can be made into a refreshing long drink with Diet Coke and ice.

MARIE'S TOP TIP

√ The portion size of rice can be really deceiving. A tblspn of boiled rice is approximately 40 calories.

√ A handy guide to remember when serving rice/pasta with your Lifestyle Plan menus is that 28g (1oz) dry weight = 85g (3oz) cooked and is approximately 100 calories. I always freeze rice into individual portions of 175g (6oz) and find this really convenient to go with the curry in a hurry, Slimtone fried rice or as a packed meal with salad.

√ Don't let that special night out sabotage your Lifestyle Plan, REMEMBER THE SLIMTONE RULE, WHEN THE KEY GOES IN THE DOOR YOUR PARTY IS OVER.

Pub Lunches

	Cals.
170g (6oz) Sirloin Steak	330
Grilled Trout	300
227g (8oz) Grilled Gammon Steak	360
Salmon Steak	300
Average Roast Dinner	450
Shepherds Pie	400
Jacket Potato	180
French Fries	350

Chinese Restaurants

	Cals.
Chicken and Mushrooms / Pineapple	375
Prawn Chop Suey	310
Beef in Oyster Sauce	345
Spare Ribs, each	140
Boiled Rice	310
Beansprouts	210

Indian Restaurants

	Cals.
Chicken Tikka	340
Chicken Tandoori	200
Onion Bhaji, each	190
Poppadum, each	65
Vegetable Samosa, each	145
Vegetable Curry	400

Italian Restaurants

	Cals.
Garlic Bread per portion	620
Cannelloni	500
Spaghetti Bolognese	720
Ravioli	510
Margherita Pizza (7")	845
Lasagne	650

The Chippie

	Cals.	Fat (g)
Chips, medium portion	500	26.0
Cod in batter, medium	445	28.0
Sausage in Batter	225	18.0
Large chicken portion (no skin)	260	6.1
Portion mushy peas/baked beans	100	nil

Corner Café	**Cals.**	**Fat (g)**
Jacket Potato with:		
Baked Beans	310	1.0
Cheese	445	21.0
Tuna & Mayo	450	9.0
Large Salad Baguette	450	2.0
Tuna Mayo Baguette	535	22.9

Coffee Bar	**Cals.**	**Fat (g)**
1 Cup of Black Coffee/Tea	nil	nil
1 Cup Cappuccino (regular)	200	16
1 Cup Café Latte (regular)	220	18
Hot Chocolate	300	28.2
Skinny Latte / Cappucino (regular)	75	nil

Alcoholic Drinks
Check out your favourite tipple…

Per 284 ml / ½ pt:	**Cals.**
Beer / Cider / Lager	90
Guinness	91
Stout e.g. Mackeson	115
Bottles: Budweiser / Becks / Foster Ice	110

Per 25 mls pub measure:	**Cals.**
Brandy / Gin / Rum / Vodka / Bacardi / Malibu	50
Tia Maria / Port	75
Sherry / Martini / Southern Comfort	80
Cointreau	85
Dooleys Toffee Liquer (50ml)	110
Baileys Irish Cream (50 ml)	155
Sheridans (50 ml)	115

Per 142 ml / 5 fl oz:	**Cals.**
Wine: Red / White / Rose	90
Champagne	105

Are you drinking enough Water?

Did you know the following facts about why we should drink our 6-8 glasses a day? (1.5 – 2 Litres)

1. Water suppresses the appetite naturally and helps the body metabolise stored fat.

Studies have shown that a decrease in water intake will cause fat deposits to increase, while an increase in water intake can actually reduce fat deposits. The kidneys can't function properly without enough water. When they don't work to capacity, some of their load is dumped on to the liver. One of the liver's primary functions is to metabolise stored fat into useable energy for the body. But, if the liver has to do some of the kidney's work, it can't operate at full throttle. As a result it metabolises less fat, more fat remains stored in the body and weight loss slows down.

2. Drinking enough water is the best treatment for fluid retention.

When the body gets less water, it perceives this as a threat to survival and begins to hold on to every drop. Water is stored in extra cellular cells (outside the cells). This shows swollen feet, legs and hands. Diuretics offer a temporary solution at best. They force out stored water along with some essential nutrients. Again, the body perceives this as a threat and will replace the lost water at the first opportunity. Thus the condition quickly returns. The best way to overcome the problem of water retention is to give the body what it needs – plenty of water. Only then will stored water be released. If you have a constant problem with water retention excess salt may be to blame. Your body will tolerate sodium only in certain concentration. The more salt you eat, the more water your system requires to dilute it. But getting rid of unneeded salt is easy – just drink more water. As it's forced through the kidneys, it takes away excess sodium. We should be eating no more than 6g of salt per day.

3. Water helps rid the body of waste.

During weight loss, the body has a lot more toxins and waste to get rid of – all that metabolised fat must be shed. Again adequate water will flush out waste.

4. Water can help relieve constipation.

When the body gets too little water, it syphons what it needs for internal sources. The colon is one primary source. Result? Constipation. But when a person drinks enough water, normal bowel functions usually return.

So far, we've discovered the following about water and weight loss:

a. The body will not function properly without enough water and can't metabolise fat efficiently.

b. Retained water shows up as excess weight.

c. To get rid of excess water you must drink more water.

d. Drinking water is essential to weight loss.

How much water is enough?

On average, a person should drink eight 227g (8oz) glasses per day. However, the over-weight person needs one additional glass for every 25 pounds of excess weight. The amount you drink also should be increased if you exercise briskly or if the weather is hot and dry. Water should preferably be cold – it's absorbed into the system more quickly than warm water. And some evidence suggests that drinking cold water can help burn calories!

BEWARE!

If you stop drinking enough water, your body fluids will be thrown out of balance again and you may experience fluid retention, unexplained weight gain and loss of thirst, plus other potential problems associated to dehydration include headaches, lethargy, lack of concentration, constipation and kidney problems.

How to Maintain Your Target Weight

Slimtone is here to help you maintain your present feeling of euphoria. To remain "on target", be guided by these simple golden rules:

1. Increase your daily calorie allowance until you reach a plateau at which you are happy. Any additional calories can be used daily but I have found that successful Slimtone target members prefer to follow the plan during the week so that they can save their indulgences for the weekend.

2. It is essential to include regular exercise in your weekly routine. Your new confidence may give you the incentive to join your local keep-fit class or don your swimsuit for a session at the pool. Or you might prefer a brisk 20 minute walk every day to provide you with the recommended level of activity. Try to fit in 30 minutes of brisk activity 5 times per week

3. Continue to follow the calorie-saving and healthy-eating advice you were given by Slimtone whilst you were losing weight. Use skimmed milk, low fat spreads and sugar free products whenever you can. Be aware when preparing meals DO NOT pre-fry meat or vegetables when cooking casseroles or soups. Use non-stick saucepans and continue to make full use of calorie-free 'fillers' in your 'Vegetable Basket'.

4. The way you look now is how you want to remain. However you must be vigilant to ensure that you do not revert back into bad habits. Keep a regular check on your weight each week. Remember it is easier to lose 2 lb than 2 stone.

5. Skipping meals can lead to uncontrolled eating later on. Always make sure that you give your metabolism a nudge by eating breakfast each day.

6. Always remember, YOU are in control. Try not to over-indulge too often. Your new positive image has been hard-won and should be cherished. Remember, the road to destruction is paved with little milestones saying 'it won't hurt me just once'.

"Taking the first step and joining Slimtone was the hardest – and I am pleased to say I have never looked back after losing over two stone and I am delighted to be featured in the exercise menu of the Lifestyle plan"

Alison Wood, Slimtone member

Slimtone Exercise Menu

It has been proven that the combination of a balanced diet together with regular exercise is the answer to a healthy Lifestyle. This section provides a simple routine which when performed on a regular basis will help tone and trim your figure.

If you have any injuries or illnesses you should consult your doctor before starting any physical activities. All exercises should be performed with suitable clothing.

These exercises should be performed at least three times a week

Warm up (Starters)

The warm up is an essential part of any exercise routine to insure that you avoid injuries. The warm up should start with activities to increase your heart rate and raise your body temperature.

You should begin your warm up routine with 5-10 minutes of aerobic exercise for example jogging / walking / stepping / exercise bike / skipping. You should start slowly and gradually increase the intensity.

Stretching

1. Arm Rotation
- Stand with your feet shoulder width apart and knees slightly bent.
- Begin by slowly rotating your arm in a clockwise direction
- You can increase the speed gradually and change direction

  Perform 20 rotations on each arm in both directions (clockwise and counter clockwise)

2. Hip rotations

- Stand with your feet just over shoulder width apart, and place your hands on your hips.
- Slowly circle your hips in a clockwise direction and increase the speed gradually.

  Perform 15 rotations clockwise and anticlockwise

3. Squats

- Stand with your feet a little wider than shoulder width apart and feet position should be pointing slightly outwards.
- Place your arms across your chest
- Slowly inhale and lower your body by moving your hips backwards until you are parallel to the floor
- Only go as far as you feel comfortable
- Exhale and drive upwards using you buttocks and quadriceps muscles.

  Perform 10 squats, rest and then another 10.

4. Quadriceps stretch
- Place a chair in front of you and place your left hand on the chair
- Hold your right foot with your right hand.
- Keep your body upright and pull your foot towards your buttocks

Perform the stretch for 20 seconds and repeat twice on each leg.

5. Hamstring stretch and calf stretch
- Sit on the floor with your legs out in front of you place a skipping rope around the ball of your right foot
- Then slowly roll backwards onto your back so that you right leg is in the air and your left leg is flat on the floor
- To increase the stretch simply pull you toes towards you.

Perform the stretch for 20 seconds and repeat twice on each leg.

Main Course

1. Press ups (Will help tone arms and upper body).
  - Lie face down on the floor.
  - Place your hands flat on the floor next to your chest.
  - Keep your legs together with the balls of your feet on the floor.
  - Exhale and push your body up until your arms straight.
  - Inhale and slowly lower your body down back to your starting position.

    *This exercise can also be performed on your knees or against a wall.
    Perform 10 repetitions and repeat 3 times*

2. Crunches (Will help strengthen abdominals and trim your tummy).
  - Lie on your back
  - Place your hands across your chest and feet flat on the floor
  - Exhale and raise your head and shoulders off the floor
  - Inhale and slowly lower your head and shoulders back onto the floor
    Perform 10 repetitions and repeat 3 times

3. Hip Extensions (Shoulder Bridge) (Excellent exercise for toning your bottom and thighs).
    - Lie on your back with feet slightly apart and flat on the floor
    - Exhale and lift your hips towards the sky
    - Inhale and slowly lower your hips back to the floor
    Perform 10 repetitions then rest repeat 3 times

4. Squats (Strengthens your upper legs, bottom and hips).
    - Stand with your feet a little more than shoulder width apart and feet position should be pointing slightly outwards.
    - Place your arms across your chest
    - slowly inhale and lower your body by moving your hips backwards until you are parallel to the floor
    - Only go as far as you feel comfortable
    - Exhale and drive upwards using you buttocks and quadriceps muscles.
    Perform 10 squats rest and repeat 3 times you can use light Dumbbells to increase difficulty.